WONDROUS STRANGE

Seven brief thoughts on new plays

CHRIS MEAD

CURRENCY PRESS
The performing arts publisher

First published in 2022
by Currency Press Pty Ltd,
PO Box 2287, Strawberry Hills, NSW, 2012, Australia
enquiries@currency.com.au
www.currency.com.au

Copyright © Chris Mead, 2022.

COPYING FOR EDUCATIONAL PURPOSES

The Australian Copyright Act 1968 allows a maximum of one chapter or 10% of this book, whichever is the greater, to be copied by any educational institution for its educational purposes provided that the educational institution (or the body that administers it) has given a remuneration notice to Copyright Agency (CA) under the Act. For details of the CA licence for educational institutions, please contact CA: 11/66 Goulburn Street, Sydney, NSW, 2000; tel: within Australia 1800 066 844 toll free; outside Australia +61 2 9394 7600; fax: +61 2 9394 7601; email: info@copyright.com.au

COPYING FOR OTHER PURPOSES

Except as permitted under the Act, for example a fair dealing for the purposes of study, research, criticism or review, no part of this book may be reproduced, stored in a retrieval system, or transmitted in any form or by any means without prior written permission. All enquiries should be made to the publisher at the above address.

Cataloguing-in-Publication data for this title is available from the National Library of Australia website: www.nla.gov.au.

Cover design Emma Vine for Currency Press.

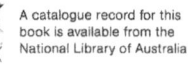 A catalogue record for this book is available from the National Library of Australia

 CHRIS MEAD is Head of Theatre at the Victorian College of the Arts, University of Melbourne. Prior to this he was Literary Director of Melbourne Theatre Company where he established Australia's most rigorous and generous new theatre writing platform, Next Stage. Other jobs have included: inaugural artistic director, Playwriting Australia; Literary Manager, Company B Belvoir; curator, Australian National Playwrights' Conference; Festival Director, International Festival for Young Playwrights; and Literary Manager, and Wharf 2LOUD Producer, Sydney Theatre Company. Recent directing credits include Ross Mueller's *A Strategic Plan* (Griffin), Richard Frankland's *Walking into the Bigness* (with Wayne Blair, Malthouse Theatre), Ian Wilding's *Rare Earth* (NIDA) and *Quack* (Griffin), and Damien Millar's *The Modern International Dead* (Griffin). Chris has a PhD from the University of Sydney, was awarded an inaugural Dramaturgy Fellowship by the Australia Council for the Arts in 2004, attended New Visions New Voices at Washington DC's Kennedy Center in 2008 and the Banff Centre for Arts and Creativity in 2019 and was a judge for Yale's Windham Campbell Award in 2015–2016. His monograph on institutional racism and outreach strategies was published by Currency House in 2008. In 2009 Chris was named as one of Sydney's 100 creative catalysts. He sat on the steering committee for the 2011 Australian Theatre Forum, on the board of Arena Theatre Company (2008–13), the artistic directorate of Hothouse Theatre (2011–2014) and the board of Theatre Network Victoria (2013–2015). He has worked closely with some of Australia's best playwrights.

CONTENTS

ACKNOWLEDGEMENTS   ix

INTRODUCTION   xi

THOUGHT ONE | The rules: What's a playwright to do?   1

THOUGHT TWO | Quality: Making it 'more gooderer'   17

THOUGHT THREE | Structure: The magic number   35

THOUGHT FOUR | Character: The source, the principle,
                        the foundation and the guide   49

THOUGHT FIVE | Dramaturgy: An ample margin   73

THOUGHT SIX | Brain soup: Story and the mind   95

THOUGHT SEVEN | Elementary particles: 'even with a
                        thought / The rack dislimns'   115

ENDNOTES   137

Currency Press acknowledges the Traditional Owners of the Country on which we live and work. We pay our respects to all Aboriginal and Torres Strait Islander Elders, past and present.

... discovering new particles is fantastic. It's very glamorous and fascinating and it means we have found new physics ... [but] we know the open questions are difficult ... Research requires a lot of patience.

—FABIOLA GIANOTTI

we're all sleeping on a sensation
bigger than us, bigger than the body

—ELLEN VAN NEERVEN

Terrible rage terrible rage

—CARYL CHURCHILL

Dès ce jour-là, la question de la vérité était posée.
(From that day on, the question of truth was posed.)

—EMILE ZOLA

HORATIO: O day and night, but this is wondrous strange!
HAMLET: And therefore as a stranger give it welcome.
There are more things in heaven and earth, Horatio,
Than are dreamt of in your philosophy.

—WILLIAM SHAKESPEARE

Si enim fallor, sum.
(Even if I err, I am.)

—AUGUSTINE OF HIPPO

Tempus edax rerum.
(Time devours all things.)[1]

—OVID

Acknowledgements

The mistakes and infelicities in all that follows belong to me alone. But I would like to thank the many, many generous and thoughtful colleagues with whom I have worked on countless plays, shows, performances and programs over the past 20 years, each contributing to my thinking on what makes plays tick. The list of playwrights to whom I owe debts is too long to note individually, but with each unique voice it has been my great joy to try and develop with them—to craft together—something of meaning, ferocity and insight.

As to my institutional colleagues, the interrogative and pragmatic clarity of Jenni Medway, Karin Farrell, Martina Murray, Jeremy Rice, Janine Snape, Sarah Thompson, Leticia Cáceres, Sarah Goodes, Sophie Boardley, Tiffany Barmann Lucas, Virginia Lovett, Brett Sheehy and Sam Strong at MTC were ever present. Prior to then it was my dream team of Amanda Macri, Susanna Dowling, Teik Kim Pok and Ben White at Playwriting Australia; Brendan Cowell, Rob Brookman and Robyn Nevin at STC; and Neil Armfield, Wesley Enoch, Rachel Healy and Lyn Wallis at Belvoir Street Theatre.

At Currency Press I would like to thank the rigorous team led by Katharine Brisbane, my tolerant and exacting editor par excellence Katie Pollock, but especially Claire Grady who read a giant earlier version of this work and remained encouraging. Thank you for your support and faith.

And at home—and this book was a product of Melbourne's extended COVID lockdowns sitting at my dining table 'desk'—I am grateful to dear friends Adam Grossetti and Naomi Rukavina; and I could not have done this without my brilliant, skeptical, intelligent and percipient daughters Harriet, Anouk and Tessa, and the extraordinary patience, eagle eyes, logic and love of my wife Syrie.

INTRODUCTION

At the end of Act One of Richard Frankland's *Walking into the Bigness* (2014), the eponymous protagonist Richard walks into the remote Aussie scrub and throws all his writing away. It is 1979. Unsure of his place in the world, evicted, with no food or even a blanket, he and his mum have hitchhiked across Australia and back again, and find themselves far from home on a road somewhere on the Nullarbor. A writer and keen observer of people, Richard figures that no-one will appreciate, let alone even read the poems, songs and stories he has been keeping in his canvas bag. This elemental, inarticulate act of rage, despair and frustration is also of course self-defeating—if he trashes his work it will be lost for good, forever unread. Out of nowhere, however, 'a willy-willy comes and picks it up mid-flight and whizzes it around'. His mother runs into the dust-storm, snatching his writing back from the wind.

Few of us will have been as destitute as fifteen-year-old Richard, the then 'skinny-ankled Koori kid', but many of us will know those feelings of fury, fear, confusion and exasperation. Richard invited me to share his stories while making that show and we discussed what it was like for him to hit metaphorical, metaphysical and literal walls, especially when it came to writing. And just as we recognise the rage, so we will also recollect that sudden feeling of wonder—

the writing coming alive, literally flying. Like the deceptively simple strategic board game Go (Chinese: 围棋; Pinyin: wéiqí), there are more possibilities, greater complexity, more surprises and 'more things in heaven and earth' when it comes to writing than we at first might suspect.[1] Like Richard, when beginning to write, we may feel anguish and joy, often simultaneously. It can also be confronting, wondrous and strange to get a glimpse of just how much we do not know, of how much there is to do, to change, to share.

These seven thoughts are written for anyone who has started the wondrous work of trying to render on stage the glory of this world, and the contradictions and complexity of being human, but then got flummoxed, fearful or second-guessed themselves. The thoughts provide a rapid overview of the most thrilling aspects— and some elementary particles—of the overturning that has taken place on stage since theatre first played in ancient Greece more than 2,500 years ago. It is an overturning that has accelerated over the past 100 years and is ongoing, making the writing of plays increasingly challenging.

That story of continual revolution is replete with volatility, insight, futility, prescience and modishness, but plays and public performance have emerged in all cultures, themselves a constant. The play script itself is a utilitarian document that seeks to capture story and the overall performance event on a piece of paper that you can hold in your hands. This makes the object of study visible, relatively easily accessible and, for many, unremarkable and uncontested. But really grasping a play, replicating its intricacy and re-imagining the physical and psychic dynamism of a play in

INTRODUCTION

performance—actor and gesture, tone and torment, pity and fear, joy and delight, surprise and shared experience—is like juggling quicksilver.

Certainties have certainly coalesced, definite conventions have accrued, and been enjoyed, and a palpable degree of conservatism has, for some, atrophied the form. But with the frequent emergence of anomalies, challenges and exceptions, orthodoxies have been upended and the form itself has been regularly resisted, rethought, rebuilt, and enjoyed anew. That formal vessel to capture and communicate the experience of human resilience in the teeth of suffering, the play—and the performance of that play in public for others to behold—has taken many, often clashing, configurations ever since.

Rendering the real, and the imagined, into dramatic form is notoriously hard to do, notwithstanding the ongoing historical flux of the form. The manner, mode and mechanics have been far from consistent, varying widely across cultures and time. Lessons have been learnt and public performance continues, sometimes with and sometimes against such lessons and, in some cultures, the freedom has been won to tell any story in any way the writer or theatre maker can imagine. However, such freedom does not necessarily make the task any easier. For some it has meant a loss of historical context, a profound opacity when it comes to knowledge of the best possible or most appropriate forms, a lack of responsibility with respect to representation or ethics, or worse, and no easy agreement on how it all coheres, that is, how it actually works. For others, limitations, rules and restrictions have seen ingenuity slyly revolutionise the form. The following essays are an attempt to chart a course between the chaos of competing theories and divergent practices, and the oversimplifications of some how-to guides.

It is not uncommon in many fields for us to develop simple methods that are convenient and useful, practices that seem natural and that explain our lives from our own point of reference. Should we alter that point of reference, however, or begin to take in the view from a different scale, we begin to observe that these perceptions are not sufficient and that to capture the multi-vocal, multiple and tangled nature of our world, we need to try harder, sometimes even to start again from scratch. The world, and us in it, is stranger, bigger, more glorious and more provocative than a three-act structure would sometimes seem to allow. In the face of such complexity we would do better to rethink the way we see the world, and at the very least to review our methods when it comes to reproducing that complexity for art and entertainment, for a play, and to open ourselves up, genuinely, to the problems and possibilities of our times. We can and must do better. These essays proffer some thoughts.

The first *Thought* looks to gain an understanding of the rules as they have been laid out since the ancient Greeks. The second focuses on one of our biggest bugbears, how we measure, assess or understand the oftentimes baffling notion of good, of quality, objectivity and the judgement involved in assessing a work of art. Mathematics and numbers are usually seen as antithetical to the making of art, but when it comes to story, a certain number have been identified as rudimentary structures and each themselves

INTRODUCTION   xv

divided into a number of component parts, ready for formulaic
reproduction. In the third *Thought* we discuss the utility of such
formulae and the questions, options and problems they generate
for construction and composition. The fourth *Thought* investigates
the recent dominance of psychology, and the vexatious nature of
psychological authenticity in the context of dramatic characters.
Dramaturgy—dark art, cudgel or closed loop—offers more than
expected and in the fifth *Thought* we assay its promise. The sixth
Thought is dedicated to the brain and recent neural discoveries.
Finally, in the seventh *Thought*, it is worth considering how
contemporary interdisciplinary fields of study are beginning to close
the gap between art and science, opening our eyes to compelling
new fields of endeavour and opportunity.

Rather than asserting universality, imposing spurious similarities
or limiting conversation—all plays do this one thing, they all follow
this certain rule, they all obey this common characteristic—these
essays celebrate change, just as plays do, themselves a dynamic,
kinetic study in transposition, modification, reconstruction,
remodelling, adjustment, reform, conversion, refinement,
reorientation and transmogrification in practice, in mind and body,
and in real time. The aim of this brief book is to hint at meaning,
scholarship and depth well beyond its scope, to inspire and impel,
pique and provoke, and reward the inquisitive. If you have ever
suspected that the theories of theatre we study, rely on or utilise
on a daily basis feel insufficient, that there must be more out there,
then this is the book for you.

Bear with me: there is vertigo, whiplash, forking paths and some thin ice ahead; but there is also insight and wonder. Please stay curious.

CHRIS MEAD
MELBOURNE, APRIL 2021

THOUGHT ONE
The rules: What's a playwright to do?

In mathematics an axiom is a fundamental rule, a rudimentary assumption of a self-evident truth. Euclid's geometry, for instance, takes certain axioms as its starting point. It is one of the most influential and useful works in history, certainly for maths, architecture and engineering, and it is unproblematic to assert: Euclid is axiomatic. He wrote the rules.

Perhaps this is the reason Raphael included Euclid in his famed early sixteenth-century Vatican Palace fresco of antiquity's greatest thinkers, *The School of Athens*. Euclid is there to Aristotle's left and Ptolemy's right, compass in hand. Above the fresco, on the roof of the actual room, two cherubs hold the command: '*Causarum Cognitio*'—seek knowledge of causes.

Indeed *The School of Athens* was Raphael's third painting of four such allegories in the one room. Each of the four walls contains a roll call of unnamed but identifiable luminaries that begins with studies in theology, then poetry, and ending with jurisprudence. For a painting at the heart of the Vatican, where the Pope had his library and signed doctrinal laws, *The School of Athens* is daring. It contains thinkers once considered heretics; wilful anachronisms; kinetic *trompe l'oeil*; in-jokes (Raphael included likenesses of his mentor Leonardo da Vinci as Plato, colleagues including Michelangelo as an isolated Heraclitus with teetering ink pot, even Raphael himself looking directly at us); a number of women including Hypatia; and a number of very non-Athenian non-Christians, most clearly Averroes (Ibn Rushd) from Islamic Cordoba and the Iranian prophet Zoroaster. He also depicted them all 'at work', that is, while the greatest thinkers may be ancient, abstract, remote and dead (mostly) white men, in this representation they are secular, actively teaching, disputatious and disparate. It is a rich and surprising contradiction—ancient but active, remote but present, no thinker dominant, with many voices jockeying, vying, arguing.

This lively, almost deafening, chorus of dissent is clarified, indeed all lines of perspective draw our attention there, at the fresco's centre and Plato and Aristotle's antithetical hand gestures. Plato's hand is pointed upwards to the heavens—receive wisdom, study the ideal and the eternal. Aristotle instead reaches forwards and down to the Earth—unearth knowledge and pursue observable things of weight and substance. Their discord is even echoed in the colour of their clothing—fire red and purple ether versus green-brown earth and watery blue.

What is Raphael's advice here? On the one hand, Raphael includes that Latin instruction *Causarum Cognitio*—most likely from Cicero's third book on oratory—above the artwork: to seek, play, argue, decode, investigate knowledge and the links between things. (Above the poetry fresco is the inscription *'Numine afflatur'*, again

THOUGHT ONE / THE RULES   3

held by cherubs—be inspired by the spirit—which is meant to signal the Christian spirit but is taken from Virgil's *Aeneid*.) On the other hand, the fresco, a paean to knowledge, is at the heart of the rule-decreeing Vatican at a height that demands that one must look up at it, literally and figuratively. Do we listen to the cherubs? Seek! Think! Or do we observe, then genuflect, to the wise men for our own edification and improvement?

Whether Raphael's intention was awe, deference or sly wit, to celebrate the past in the present, to mock, overwhelm or dazzle the hand that commissioned him, the ultimate lesson of this artwork is nevertheless reasonably clear: look up and learn from the Pantheon how to do things axiomatically, the true and correct way, their way. Most importantly it serves as a reminder that, like the militant Pope Julius II who commissioned the fresco itself, they wrote the rules. If there is a key axiom here about thinking and doing, this is arguably it: regardless of whether we are secretly laughing at them, the rules are already written, self-evident, masculine, imposing, set.

Starting from scratch with anything is tough, a new work of art or philosophy especially so. Sometimes it is just easier to start by following the rules, to make a thing according to the authority of someone who knows better. And at the centre of playwriting, as in the centre of Raphael's towering, magisterial painting about the nature of wisdom itself, is the authority of Aristotle. As in so many other disciplines, Aristotle wrote 'the rulebook' on theatre.

Aristotle is revered in theatre because his *Poetics* was considered 'as infallible as the Elements of Euclid'.[1] It is hard not to admire the genius of Aristotle (384–322 BCE) not only because he examined almost every subject possible during his lifetime, but because he made significant contributions to those subjects. He appraised the natural world—anatomy, astronomy, economics, embryology, geography, geology, meteorology, physics and zoology—and the philosophical one—aesthetics, ethics, logic, metaphysics, politics, psychology, rhetoric and theology—and tutored a young Alexander the Great while also configuring what we would now call education, foreign relations and literature. According to Diogenes Laërtius, noted biographer of classical philosophers, Aristotle had a lisp and skinny legs, was a fancy dresser, and his combined extant works effectively constitute an encyclopedia. This in the knowledge that the vast majority of his studies have been lost (only 31 remain of approximately 200 treatises).[2]

Aristotle's analysis of the dramatic experience in his work *Poetics* (c.335 BCE) continues to form the basis for conversations about drama, theatre, plays and literary criticism, most particularly his dissection of a play's hierarchy of working components.[3] Primary in his order of functional importance is plot, followed by characterisation, then rhetoric or reasoning, diction, verbal expression or idiom, style, completeness and irrationalities, contradictions and errors, then finally actors and performance, spectacle and the visual aspects of a play.

Aristotle sought to differentiate plays from epic poetry, to demarcate their differences despite their similarities: in his day both meant storytelling directly to an audience. In his analysis of their distinctness he introduced a number of concepts that are still often considered axiomatic: *hamartia, muthos, agon, mimesis, diegesis*, *peripeteia*, *anagnorisis*, *telos*, *stichomythia*, *catharsis* and *eudaimonia*. There are many more.[4]

Following Plato, Aristotle noted that epic poetry (such as the *Iliad* or the *Odyssey*) employed *diegesis*, that is, storytelling or narration, as opposed to theatre, which relied instead on *mimesis*, that is, imitating, representing, showing or making a likeness of.[5] Aristotle, however, advanced a new notion, that the experience of tragedy, unlike that of poetry, led to the elimination, purgation or purification of troubling emotions—*catharsis*. This purgation occurred because of tragedy's truthfulness, seriousness (or elevation, *spoudaios*) and tight structuring of events. Tragedy summoned difficult emotions in us but, in Aristotle's estimation, it was through *catharsis* that we transcended the fear and terror that the play conjured, ultimately feeling pleasure. Beyond that, we gained a deeper understanding of the world as a result of experiencing the dramatic tragedy played before us.[6] In watching it, we may even have learnt something.

Aristotle's central contention was that plays, ideally, were powerful, transformative and instructive. They evoked intoxicating emotions because we witnessed characters—better versions of ourselves—making choices, mistakes and resolutions that in turn both defined and refined their characters, their *ethos*. The Greek word is close but not synonymous with our notion of character and Aristotle used it to indicate an ongoing internal battle between will, choice, intent and nous.[7]

For Aristotle, tragedies all follow a similar pattern. Firstly, there is a protagonist, or 'first sufferer', who pushes the contest or struggle (the *agon*) forward, thereby testing their virtue. This act of testing, not as an abstract concept but as deployed in the field as it were, forms the basis of the play as a whole.[8] Secondly, the virtuous protagonist then makes a miscalculation, or demonstrates an erring waywardness (*hamartia*) followed by an unexpected reversal of fortune (*peripeteia*).[9] Finally, they suffer through the resulting dreadful events, but ultimately recognise a greater truth (*anagnorisis*). Through their suffering and death—it is a tragedy after all—we in the audience are transformed, having experienced *catharsis*.

In Aristotle's diagnosis, for the tragedy to be successful the audience must find the character's choices and actions credible, and the events plausible, selectively condensed and cleverly structured into a plot or *muthos*.[10] When the protagonist makes their mistake or mistakes, we recognise that while they aren't real, their actions are nevertheless likely, credible and distressing, and we are moved by this exhibition of human agency, suffering and fallibility. Tragedy, for Aristotle, engages consuming, terrifying emotions that, once we reflect on the choices made by the characters—and because it is a work of art and not actually taking place—drive genuine critical reflection on the challenges and responsibility of doing good in the world. For Aristotle, this *catharsis* is decisive in our ongoing struggle towards happiness—*eudaimonia*—or living well and being well-favoured.

Aristotle's was an ideal case, an ideal play. How much theatre had he actually seen? How many audiences had he sat in? Scholars of antiquity have noted that the *Poetics* was actually rarely read in classical times and it is certainly true to say that very few plays that have come down to us conform to his ideal. In addition, the plays he valorised and used as models were first staged well before his birth. The great tragedian Euripides had died 40 years before Aristotle was born, Aeschylus 80 years prior, with *Oedipus* and *Antigone* first produced 100 years earlier than the probable date of the collation of the *Poetics*. Aristotle scrutinised the storylines of play-texts without context; his only references to actors, performances or the stage are in passing; and his investigative focus is on tragedy's form on the page and its effect on an abstract audience's psyche, not on theatre practices or the sweat behind the masks.[11] As a proto-scientist, he collected, detected and classified only a very narrow data sample— the play texts of fifth-century Athens—and he drew conclusions based on that.

But his analysis was never intended as a how-to guide or a set of hard rules. He was interested in the form, nature and value of play composition, and he offered a functional anatomy for plays. Aristotle scrutinised finished plays in order to identify common patterns and to settle two arguments. First, he looked to clarify the evident difference between poetry and plays. Second, he wanted to mount a case against Plato's denunciation of theatre.

In his dramatic dialogue, *Republic*, Plato recounted Socrates' argument that art was a copy of a copy (a secondary imitation of the divine), twice removed from the truth, and thus both morally suspect and ethically reprehensible. More specifically, witnessing a theatrical tragedy made citizens susceptible to corrosive despair, ultimately corrupting their souls. For Socrates (c.470–399 BCE), theatre shattered subjectivity, or rather, the longed-for unity of the soul, either because it encouraged citizens (in the audience) to imagine others' points of view or to imagine multiple psyches at once. As a result, according to Socrates, theatre should have no place in an ideal city-state. Aristotle's *Poetics*, however, formulated a very different argument.

For Aristotle more generally, we are what we do: action is the key to our character. Plays consist entirely of action, that is, all that takes place in them, all that we witness, are the choices a fictional character makes (setting plays well apart from other art forms). It is not a character's whole life or its overall quality that is fundamental to a play, not whether there is, or is not, *hamartia*, *perepetiea* or *anagnorisis*, perfect diction or meter, but rather what a character does in trying to achieve a certain goal, the actions they take to alleviate their suffering. This is what Aristotle described as dramatic action. Aristotle identified this as the heart of theatre.

And from this astute Aristotelian observation we can deduce a startling axiom: that theatre is a study in change, instability, making, striving, seeking and remaking. In epic poetry the story is already written, but in a play we watch the protagonist make their choices in real time—perhaps they will pick differently this time? Indeed the *Poetics*—not actually Aristotle's title but one given to it later—derives from the word for 'making', a perhaps unexpected title for a rulebook on finished plays. It hints at an art form that is more process than outcome, an experience that is in flux and unpredictable. Taken together, action and making capture theatre's essence—change, balance and re-balance, assembly and re-assembly. Far from being something rule-bound, a static but replaceable literary checklist, here theatre is fundamentally alive to change. In this sense then plays are active, they bring something into being, are about action and not yielding to rules, about doing, failing, and failing better. A good reminder of this is that the Greek origin of the word drama is *dran* or *drāo*—to do, act, make, perform.

This supple understanding of a play, however, was not the approach taken by a writer just 60 years after Raphael's painting of his great fresco when Aristotle's text—missing from the Western canon since late Roman times—was rediscovered thanks to centuries of Islamic scholarship. Since Rome's collapse a millennium of Western erudition had centred on Biblical texts and their interpretation so when, during the Renaissance, texts including Aristotle's were re-examined, its 'laws' were extracted and clear rules brought forth. Indeed Lodovico Castelvetro's 1570 'translation' into Italian (which was burnt for heresy) and then his later 1576 'translation and explanation' took Aristotle's slim volume and expanded it from barely 50 pages (in my Penguin Classics edition) to 1,000 pages.

Although scholars from the 1520s on had begun to boil Aristotle's *Poetics* down to three rules, it was Castelvetro who formalised, in a prolix and definitive way, what have since come to be known as the Three Unities—perhaps theatre's most enduring 'law'. Castelvetro himself made quite a number of his own extrapolations—tragedy had six qualitative parts, history two, plot had eight requirements, comedy four classes, narrative and dramatic modes differed for six key reasons, and so on—but from Aristotle he deduced that a play should have common-sense rules that would allow uneducated audiences to enjoy it without suspending their disbelief.

The first of his rules, Place, was that plays should take place in only the one room, because of the physical limitations of the stage. The second was that a play's narrative should also occur only in real time. This was because audiences, according to Castelvetro, would not believe that a play had taken place over multiple days (or places) when their senses told them otherwise: they 'cannot endure more than one course of the sun over the earth'. Plus an audience, in Castelvetro's opinion, would find shorter plays more convenient, especially when it came to thinking about how long some extant plays were—which also led to him recommending the use of few, if any, sub-plots.

What is perhaps most curious about Castelvetro is that he was less precious about observing Aristotle's only actual call to unity—that of one plot or of a unified central Action, 'an orderly arrangement of parts'—than for demanding fidelity to his two interpolations, the supposed unities of Place and Time. While Aristotle does mention time in passing when discussing unity—a play's length should be 'easily embraced by the memory'—he does not mention place at all. For Castelvetro, however, the unity of action was more a suggestion than a rule. To his thinking, no-one should restrict the imagination of the poet because, actually, the 'multitude' liked the miraculous and an 'astonishing event can make the action more terrible and more fitted to arouse compassion'.[12]

Castelvetro warned that any who held other notions 'should beware of opposing the authority of Aristotle', even though he had consistently done so. While basking in the authority of Aristotle, Castelvetro freely adapted his work. It was a rhetorical sleight of hand practised for the next couple of hundred years and, while perhaps it lent some prestige and reflected classical virtue to the always morally suspect theatre, it also saddled writers with a normative literary straitjacket and an imposed 'theory' of plays that set itself well above the exigencies of playhouses.

The Three Unities were invoked in England within ten years of Castelvetro, courtesy of playwright, wit and courtier Philip Sidney (1554–1586). Indeed references to the 'Lawes of Poetry' of Time, Place and Action crop up repeatedly in Elizabethan, Jacobean and Caroline plays, including in Shakespeare's, but most especially in the work of classicist and autodidact Ben Jonson (1572–1637). That the rules were consistently broken or ignored did not stop writers making references to them because of their value as a classical shield, as literary misdirection from attacks by Puritans and as a demonstration of their erudition, but also as a way for a playwright to beg the audience's favour and forgiveness.

Spanish playwright Lope de Vega (1562–1635) wrote a long poem in 1609 to apologise for ignoring the 'laws', though mostly to mock them. French playwright Pierre Corneille (1606–1684) wrote a whole disquisition he called an '*examens*' on the Unities in 1660. He exhibited his deference to Aristotle, and to the all-powerful theocratic French state with its newfound love of morally upright theatre; but his book also included some workarounds for two of the Three Unities. Restoration England's pre-eminent man of letters John Dryden (1631–1700) praised playwrights who 'dress'd in all the ornaments and colours of the Ancients', especially so if the rules were 'observ'd in every regular play; namely of Time, Place and Action'; but he gave Shakespeare a free pass despite his repeated violations of the Unities. A century later Samuel Johnson (or Dr Johnson, 1709–1784) too discussed the Unities of Time and Place, though he reckoned they gave 'more trouble to the poet than pleasure to the auditor', and also forgave Shakespeare his trespasses.

The brilliant bluestocking and literary critic Elizabeth Montagu (1718–1800), however, went further. She offered a corrective, wanting to keep critics and their highbrow philosophising out of theatres. A contemporary of Johnson's, she was aware that Shakespeare, for the 'more learned, deep and sober critics', had one considerable disadvantage: 'his portraits are not of the Greek or the Roman school'. For Montagu, connoisseurs and the 'literati' formed their acquaintance with 'mankind in the library' and 'not in the street, the camp or the village' where most humans lived and worked. The literati saw characters as busts from 'learned museums' and dismissed Shakespeare's plays as 'monstrous and ill-constructed' because of their deviation from the Unities. For Montagu, however, such a view was peevish and pedantic and simply could not explain how Shakespeare's plays worked 'better than anyone has ever done'.

In 1863 a German playwright and novelist set playwriting rules for would-be writers without recourse to a 'learned museum' at all. Dr Gustav Freytag (1816–1895) claimed allegiance to Aristotle, and, like him, used a handful of plays as a guide, mining them for a new set of instructions not taken from high literary classical culture. He placed his faith in his own technique and a newfound—for literature—reliance on technical data and diagrams. Freytag observed that all plays (by the five writers whose plays he mined—Sophocles, Shakespeare, Lessing, Goethe and Schiller) used a 'pyramidal structure'. This 2D up-and-down, big dipper shape has since become so ubiquitous that it appears as gospel in any internet search for dramatic structure. He eschewed literary theory, Greek words and Renaissance edicts, and dismissed the 'strife' of the Three Unities, preferring practical tips and a five-step structure: introduction, rise, proportionate climax, catastrophe or downturn and conclusion. Freytag's book *Technique of the Drama* (translated into English in 1894) provided readers with a checklist of tasks to deliver a successful play. Indeed it opens

This 2D up–and–down, big dipper shape has since become so ubiquitous that it appears as gospel in any internet search for dramatic structure

with a disavowal of absolute rules, offering technical education and practical knowledge instead. It, far more than his plays and novels, was a bestseller.

Since the great flowering of Athenian theatre, a play's coherence and imaginary forces have perplexed, vexed and enchanted writers, critics and audiences. When theatre turned professional and institutional from the late sixteenth century right across Europe, accepted but malleable theatre conventions shifted conclusively. Customs and hand-me-down touchstones morphed and ossified into supposed classical principles, then rigid rules. And this was a first: playwrights having to justify their plays—in dialogue and in standalone ex-post-facto treatises—according to apparent axioms of dramatic composition. The roar of the groundlings diminished as theatre adhered to the wishes of the cognoscenti. Aristotle opened a fault line between practitioners and theorists, then Castelvetro underlined a divide between the educated and the 'crude multitude'. The subsequent 300- to 400-year debate about poetic laws masked a deeper malaise: a steady focus on the relationship between text and authority, over and above the relationship between players, a play and the audience. The debate suggested that plays were not a porous whole but mere collections of parts, contraptions and devices, either correctly or incorrectly fitted together. Far from opening drama up, playwriting rules closed possibilities down—catastrophe indeed.

Perhaps the most significant shift recently in 'rules' was captured about 20 years ago with the publication of Hans-Thies Lehmann's book *Postdramatic Theatre* (written in German in 1999, it was translated into French, Japanese, Slovenian, Croatian, Polish and Persian/Farsi before appearing in English in 2006).[13]

He sought to theorise the practices common amongst some European theatre makers—directors such as Einar Schleef, Frank Castorff, Heiner Müller, Klaus-Michael Grüber, Jan Fabre and Romeo Castellucci, and companies Forced Entertainment and the American Robert Wilson, but harking back in particular to Antonin Artaud and Jerzy Grotowski—and their profound break with traditional theatre semiotics. Much of it centred around the rejection of the primacy of the text. According to Lehmann, a rupture had

THOUGHT ONE / THE RULES   15

taken place, with older orthodoxies of narrative, text, action and character fragmenting increasingly into newer methodologies and practices favouring bricolage, pure theatricality, architectronics, unalloyed physicality and heightened ritual. Theatre that he termed 'postdramatic' superseded text in favour of a scenic, communal dynamic and 'the emphatically or monumentally accentuated ostentation of the presentation'.[14]

The book celebrates a perhaps final severing of theatre from literary drama and its arcane rules, with the emergence instead of theatre as performance. In a revision for the English version, Lehmann reincorporated 'text' (and redressed an unintended hierarchical binary) through the plays of Sarah Kane. Her plays, while deeply literary, also rejected the old rules of mimesis, illusion, action, plot and the unities, upholding instead non- and anti-narrative devices, fragmented character, shared experience and an immersion in theatre's disparate heterogeneity.

There is one classical axiom that I do hold close, and if I could paint like Raphael I would depict cherubs carrying it. The rule belongs to Roman poet Horace: *'decipimur specie recti'*, that is, we are often misled—or undone—by the illusion of correctness or the appearance of rectitude. Horace, like Aristotle, is reputed to have written a definitive guide to playwriting, *Ars Poetica*. It, however, is no guide at all. It is written as a letter of advice to the Piso family, a family that did not exist. Horace claims to be an authority on drama, but it was a form he never practised. And for a piece about poetic unity it has no title (another title conferred after the fact); is full of digressions and vague, contradictory advice that is mostly coined in the negative; and principally suggests that poetry should not be attempted at all, especially by non-poets.

Horace's advice is that you cannot trust advice, most particularly when trying to be right, or when following the rules. As far as dramatic axioms go, it is—like Euclid's geometry—elementary, a rudimentary assumption of a self-evident truth.

THOUGHT TWO

Quality: Making it 'more gooderer'

In a varied pre-theatre career, I once worked for social services with young people who had removed themselves, or been removed, from school and family life. We would do mundane activities together—go to the park, play board games, buy the shopping, not eat junk food—to keep them socialised, healthy and active. One of these young people loved playing chess. They also loved the movies. Sometimes we would play chess before a movie, sometimes it was a movie then chess—I carried a chess travel pack. We usually played in the food court at a local mall and the young person would beat me every time. I like to think it was just because they had learnt to play with their back row pieces in a unique order (from the outside edge: rook, bishop, knight, rather than the customarily arranged rook, knight, bishop) but they were just better than me.

Any opening gambits I played were confounded by their simple piece-swap. Later, when discussing films, they would want to know if the proposed movie was going to be 'more gooderer' or 'more betterer' than their favourite. As with the chess pieces, I tried to correct them, this time about grammar. Again they pushed back:

why was my way more gooderer than their way? Two simple acts and my notions of good, of proper order, of received rules, were overthrown. Was their version of chess bad? Was their question about relative merits no good? Suddenly, certain rudimentary aspects of our social construct, maybe even the social contract itself, were in tatters. Shouldn't I know what was good? Wasn't that my job?

Ask anyone for their best theatre experience and a memory or two usually springs to mind, after some mental gymnastics—good for them, good for the audience, good for art and posterity? Ask anyone for their worst theatre experience, however, and the stories tumble out unfiltered: it was infuriating, it was appalling, it was risible, it was so, so terrible. Is this just *schadenfreude* or is there something significant in the fact that we are more compelled by the bad, than thoughtful and circumspect about the good? Recent studies have shown that laughing at others' misfortune—on the spectrum from slapstick, to justice being meted out, to dehumanisation—may be an evolutionary strategy that activates the brain's reward systems, perhaps strengthening our pain thresholds. Similarly scholars argue that we remember the bad times (more so when young apparently) over the good because they may have adaptive value, lessons to help us better survive.

There is little in life as miserable as sitting through a dismal show, but it won't actually kill or maim us. Is there any real cost (other than ticket price and one's time) of a bad play? Regardless, the experience itself is palpable and our resolve, and our certainty in our own taste, is reinforced the longer the perceived badness goes on. For some it may even encourage the tallying of faults,

THOUGHT TWO | QUALITY

errors, egregious lapses in judgement, poor lines and execrable decisions, weak ideas and deficient artistry, and so on. Our growing compendium of the bad, even in a new play reading that lasts barely an hour, often runs to many volumes. As the failures accrete, it's surprising how easily categories, sub-categories and reasons gather in the mind. What is this certainty, who is this inner critic and why is it so easy to judge? What part do education, taste, competence, compassion, morality, universal rules or socialisation play? What do we know, what is belief and what is assertion? And is it really so easy to register the good?

When I was seventeen years old, I was sure I knew what was good. An amateur production of Nick Enright's play *On the Wallaby* blew my mind. The stage was split in two: opposite prompt side offered a naturalistic landscape, a family doing it tough; prompt side, however, was a running meta-commentary performed by actors, not 'characters', a space in which the actors discussed the wider social context of the play and the good, bad, or maddening decisions the characters made. For a suburban neophyte, this meta-commentary was a revelation.

> What is this certainty, who is this inner critic and why is it so easy to judge others?

Then, as a nineteen-year-old uni student watching *Cloud Nine* by Caryl Churchill, I realised there was a new good in town. That ideas could be built into and explored through the very form of the play itself was breathtaking—especially in this thrilling, funny, consistently provocative and deeply shocking play. Then, at 22, it was the work of The Sydney Front and their playful exploration of the actor–audience relationship that was pivotal in my realignment of good. In the company's final work, *Passion*, the audience 'made' the bulk of the show: we seemingly crucified one audience member, after dressing them in a clown suit and making them ride a tricycle up a ramp (a representation of Calvary!). After their 'death' the theatre went to a hard blackout and that moment of disorientation was followed immediately by a light blasting through a grave-shaped cut-out in the ceiling. The light, however, was increasingly blocked by dirt, shovelled by performers in the ceiling across the gradually diminishing grave-like rectangle. As the light slowly weakened, we were again in the dark, though a very gentle misty rain did fall. These shows challenged everything that I thought I knew about the theatre. In trying to quantify these experiences—why and how they were so good—all I knew was that there were great ideas, executed well and enjoyed.

Do my experiences accord with proper metrics? I liked these shows but did my taste have any other than a subjective, arbitrary basis, indicative only of my own limited ways of seeing and interpreting? Chatting once outside a London theatre with a brilliant, renowned theatre director and an emerging playwright, the freelance playwright asked the salaried director what kind of plays they were looking for. Comedies? Short plays? Tragedies? The director took a moment and then said, deadpan: good ones. But what does good mean, look or sound like?

This brief foyer discussion reminded me of Polonius discussing plays with Hamlet: 'tragedy, comedy, history, pastoral, pastoral-comical, historical-pastoral, tragical-historical, tragical-comical-historical-pastoral, scene individable, or poem unlimited'. Act Two Scene Two of *Hamlet* is astonishing, the longest in the play, in the longest of any of Shakespeare's plays, it is concerned mostly with theatre, with Hamlet even explaining why plays are good. He acknowledges that a particular play 'pleased not the million' but that, for him, it was 'well digested in the scenes', delivered with 'as much modesty as cunning'. It had 'no sallets in the lines to make the matter savory' (that is, a good play contains nothing to over-spice it, like salted meat and egg) and, according to Hamlet, the writer employed 'an honest method' that was wholesome and sweet, more 'handsome than fine'. He figures that, in this light, his own story possesses a powerful 'motive and cue for passion' that would indeed 'cleave the general ear', drive the guilty mad, terrify the innocent, confound the unknowing, and amaze the rest. For Hamlet, and Shakespeare, plays find people 'strook to the soul', so much so that audiences may even then proclaim 'their malefactions' as a result of having watched the play.[1]

It is as good a list as any of the qualities to look for in why one play is better than another; and certainly what might make plays good. Re-reading Hamlet's list did not help when I first became curator of the Australian National Playwrights' Conference and needed to assess hundreds of play submissions. Playwrights entered for a very limited number of development slots and I wanted to assure them that their plays were being read and assessed fairly. As a result I created a tick-a-box form to accompany the reading of each play, immediately acknowledging its shortcomings: it was reductive; it applied uniform standards to a diverse and divergent field; it contained only two pages of criteria; it sort of resembled a teen magazine quiz about love and star signs; it dissected a complex document; and it narrowed a play down to a score.

I also knew, however, that it was a start towards regularity and objectivity: it meant there was a degree of correspondence in the way assessors would read and discuss plays; it was indeed a series of correctives and reminders on detailed reading for assessors; it contained three dissonant value systems to encourage assessors to pause before committing their initial thoughts as their final thoughts; it was only the first tool in a range of systems, checks and balances in the winnowing process; it was not a replacement for discussion and debate of new plays; and it gave each play a score, making them rankable. Maybe it was anti-intellectual and anti-art but it did guarantee transparency and accountability in play assessment. The form tried to capture gut response, technical competency, and the urgency, reach, originality and ambition of the work; and to condense all that into a score and recommendation as to whether it should be read a second time. It was an attempt to capture 'good'. As limited and limiting as it was, more than fifteen years later, I still see versions of that form across the country as a play assessment tool. Clearly other people struggle with objectivity, subjectivity, clarity and uncertainty, in sorting the good from the bad.

Is the list itemised by Hamlet, and Shakespeare, as good or better than Aristotle's? Is it more or less useful than observing the Three Unities? Following Freytag's pyramid? Cribbing from Horace?

THOUGHT TWO | QUALITY

Filling out my form? This question of degrees of quality—declaring something good—is a core part of our work, yet, while it remains hazy for us, audiences know what they like, booing, walking out or giving standing ovations without hesitation.[2] Is a play's 'goodness' about promise, its literary qualities, the audience response, tickets sold, moral lessons, great roles or staging challenges? What matrix, or lattices, should be deployed to make a judgement on multiple plays' qualities?

It sounds like we are talking about aesthetics. But aesthetics can describe an attitude, objects, a kind of judgement, experience and value, so what actually is it? Fully developed as a branch of philosophy over 300 years ago, aesthetics was a mode of study invented to capture all that we have so far discussed: an ideal science of what can be sensed, experienced or imagined. Today aesthetics sits at the contested threshold of objectivity, normativity and subjectivity, caught in their mutual antagonism. It manages the competing demands of philosophy, sociology, religion, education, history, feminism, cultural studies and literary criticism; people, places and things; intention and the Intentional Fallacy. First, it pursues the nature of good; second, it scrutinises the indicators that signify good, testing, assessing and quantifying those indicators; and finally, those markers themselves shift and morph across space, time, culture and class, even across the time it takes to write and produce a single play, itself an aesthetic act.

Immanuel Kant (1724–1804) critically, methodically and austerely excavated notions of taste, beauty, pleasure, virtue and good in his 1790 work *Critique of the Power of Judgement*.[3] This work was and remains definitive. Kant examined the relationship between values, the sublime and morality, with aesthetics conclusively confirmed as a separate and distinct branch of philosophy. Other thinkers had begun to explore taste, genius, poetry, painting and beauty in the eighteenth century, falling on either side of two approaches: that beauty and taste depend on experience and individual mental representations; or that they depend on universal principles and logical constants. Either way, it was clear that art—drama, literature, sculpture, painting, music—was a special vehicle for the expression of important truths, required close study and, for Kant, was tethered to reason and moral laws.

However, Kant argued that the attempt to create an exact science out of judging beauty was ultimately futile. A particular insight of his was not to concentrate on defining beauty, value or taste, its affect or effect, but to analyse the act of judging it. In Kant's view, sense judgements could not be trusted and revolved around inclinations not determinations. Because of this he sought to interrogate the relationship between universal truths and sensory experiences without positing that it was either all in the mind or simply reliant on abstract maxims. Bringing semantics, logic, metaphysics, moral philosophy and epistemology together, Kant argued that in judging we used the abstract and the immediate simultaneously. Indeed the act of judging, in his view, transpired because our imaginations brought reason and sense perception together through the faculties of understanding and sensibility. Kant placed the imagination at the centre of our perceiving of, and thinking on, the world. Indeed judgement was the cognitive faculty that united otherwise disparate cerebral systems—intuition, imagination, conceptualisation and reason—into rational self-consciousness. For Kant, to be a rational human is to judge.

Kant insisted that aesthetic judgements found validity in three interrelated stabilising movements: in intersubjectivity (despite personal and private judgement, people's taste and evaluations often align); in a measure of disinterestedness (when we recognise something as beautiful but do not want to possess it, i.e., desire does not distort our appreciation of the object of study); and because of their moral significance. Critical reflective judgement promoted the highest good for Kant, bridging a chasm between nature's mechanisms and humanity's virtuous, scientific purpose.

While Kant's conception of the role of the imagination and its relationship to sensibility, his notion of disinterestedness, and the absence of any commentary from him on emotion, have all been flashpoints for scholars, his theory that judgement united disparate thoughts remains rich, complex and, while close to paradoxical, illuminating. For Kant the act of judging had a binding function—a harmonious collision of feeling, imagination, reason and intuition— that he called 'free play'. Rather than fixing a concept to a thing, or a thing to a concept, Kant's contention was that the pleasure we experience in judging beauty relates to this free play, like the surprise of discovering the unexpected. Free play is possible, for Kant, because it takes place 'without concept' and with none of the constraints that apply to our other faculties, the imagination being in a state of 'lawfulness without a law'.

Kant's central argument that beautiful things—in nature or

made by humans—are models, not for slavish imitation but as inspiration for more artistic production, is itself an incitement to further discourse. For Kant, beautiful art requires: 'genius' (not a person so much as the union of imagination and understanding); new content; new forms for the expression of this content; freedom for the artist; and imaginative stimulation for the audience.[4]

Looking for answers and against my expectations, Kant pointed out that judgement was neither easy nor certain, neither static nor already resolved. His *Critique of Judgement*—just one part of a much larger project reconfiguring and stabilising teleology, morality and reason—considered judgement inchoate, uncertain, playful, oscillating, vibrant. There is a structure to it but it consists, in its essence, in movement. The imagination is a generator and conductor of new ideas that shuttle ceaselessly between our understanding and our sensibility, our capacity for reason and finally towards a deeper socially engaged sense of good. Judgement, for Kant, exists as a point of tension between conflicting faculties, paradoxically, both free and lawful. While neurologically and philosophically debatable, and certainly relentlessly contested, Kant nevertheless offers a surprising measure of activity, of liveness and indeterminacy, to judgement. As with re-reading Aristotle, far from finding Kant sober, fixed and secure, it required a realignment of my thinking. That, and that our focus must shift from a concern about good to the problem of *judging* good.

When I was at Sydney Theatre Company and administered the Patrick White Playwrights' Award, I encountered this problem head-on. Frustrated at the shortcomings of reading plays in bulk,

I introduced what I termed the Control Play, a play each assessor would read and evaluate with other anonymous entries using my form. The control play itself was ambitious, took as its subject a then hot-button issue and, while it had flaws, was thoughtfully planned and efficiently executed. How did it fare? The scores ranged from 21 to 42 out of 50 (I scored it at 35). Over three years, three control plays and hundreds of entries, a 20-point standard deviation was a constant. Here, clearly, though instability and movement were theoretically intriguing, practically it created a problem with judging plays and provided no easy agreement on quality.

Kant noted, in passing, that language itself may not be able to contain aesthetic ideas, or even make them legible.[5] That there might be a problematic, slippery relationship between thought and action, or language and judgement, has since occupied quite a few philosophers, including Friedrich Nietzsche, Sigmund Freud, Edmund Husserl, Ludwig Wittgenstein, Walter Benjamin, Theodor Adorno, Michel Foucault, Julia Kristeva, Hélène Cixous, Jacques Derrida and Luce Irigaray. Part of the problem in thinking on aesthetics, they argued, is not only that the question of whether sense impressions can be rational, true or correct remains unresolved, but that language itself, while extraordinary, also gives rise to speculation, abstraction and falsity. With the ability to describe comes the ability to dissemble; as we share, consider, understand, imagine and question, so we can also use reason, knowledge, thinking, heuristics and language to repress, distort, manipulate and misrepresent, and do so with axiomatic assuredness. We must, they argue, pay close attention to language's historical sedimentation. What of this linguistic turn? Perhaps language cannot guarantee meaning and correctness, truth and goodness, but only giddying relativism. They ask, thinking especially on the course of the twentieth century, whether you can assert any measure of authority without exercising authoritarianism. Another of language's potential dangers, they insist, is letting value relate to a standard that is also the source of that standard.

Given the vicissitudes of language, it is to literary criticism then that we should turn, briefly. Certainly since Plato and Plotinus, but especially over the past 300 years, writers and critics have sought to derive a degree of certainty from aesthetic judgements. When in 1924 pioneering literary critic I.A. Richards surveyed the contribution of critics to the simple questions of value and a work of art's relative merits he was a little despondent that, despite the brilliance, wit and genius of generations of artists, there was so little of value or merit written by critics about why or how to achieve this:

> A few conjectures, a supply of admonitions, many acute isolated observations, some brilliant guesses, much oratory and applied poetry, inexhaustible confusion, a sufficiency of dogma, no small stock of prejudices, whimsies and crotchets, a profusion of mysticism, a little genuine speculation, sundry stray inspirations, pregnant hints and random *aperçus*; of such as these, it may be said without exaggeration, is extant critical theory composed.[6]

If a Cambridge don couldn't work it out, where does that leave the rest of us? Perhaps, after Derrida, we should embrace what he termed *différance* or suspension before judgement, an immersion in irresolvable contradictions to resist dogmatic thinking, privileging variability over hierarchy, engaging in active interpretation.

From the previous *Thought* we might remember that Plato and Aristotle claimed that art was an imitative skill (sculpture, music or visual art as imitative of nature, the human form or human emotion; with theatre and poetry imitative of lived events), a view that held sway until the eighteenth and nineteenth centuries. Judging art therefore required assessing how well it imitated eternal truths and accepted wisdom. Eighteenth and nineteenth century 'men of letters' by contrast offered instead a radical new notion of art as self-expression, an externalisation of an artist's inner vision, with art made and consumed for pleasure, which in itself could be considered good. The judgement of art was transformed by these critics, for as they measured so-called 'genius', passion, national aspiration and art for art's sake, they sidelined traditional domestic arts and crafts, with artistic practice itself bifurcating along class lines into high and popular culture but also into private and public realms. This excluded much activity, and many people, from the 'legitimate' art world. Indeed some Romantic critics argued that far from art being imitative of nature, artistic expression, by its very elevated features, ennobled its subject. The frame and the form, decorative, filigreed and ornate, had itself become the story.

Twentieth century Modernist critics sharpened this valorisation of form but dismissed the Romantic embrace of 'spontaneous overflow of powerful feelings'.[7] By the 1920s this approach to art analysis came under attack from what was termed the New Criticism. The New Critics eschewed generalising about works of art, opting instead for a close, 'neutral' reading of each work, with the artist's intentions and biography of little interest to the critic. By the cessation of World War II, criticism itself exploded to include multiple influences and myriad lines of inquiry: Freudian interpretations, alienation, Futurism, feminist critiques, cultural materialism, the incorporation of myth and ritual, post-modernism, structuralism, post-structuralism, New Historicism, deconstruction, Queer Theory and post-colonialism, to name a few. In the simplest of reductions, criticism and judgement were no longer focused on pursuit of the good, genius or neutrality but were now fractured, splintered, specific and multivalent. What of power? What of class, and relationships to the means of production? What of race? What of gender? What of hierarchy, violence and who has the upper hand? What of those who cannot or who choose not to speak? What of the subaltern? What of desire? What of the Other? What of the body? What of erotogeneity? What of the so-called inadequate and disqualified? What of hybridity and double-vision?

Some readers may be familiar with some of these questions, others may know the philosophers and problems to which they allude; still more may be frustrated or even overwhelmed. After proposing to discuss value and what good might mean, or be, we have instead become tangled in questions, dropped into radical doubt and become mired in double- or even triple-speak. What of a dependable intellectual scaffolding, a unifying and unified practice or an essential hypothesis? With such certainties rejected, discontinuity, provisionality and a relentless multiple barrage of self-critical reflection are preferred. This leaning away from definitive meaning, grand concepts and confident answers might initially feel annoying, a cop out, a diversion or a real time waster. I would suggest, however, that it is critical for us.

First, by holding off answering unanswerable questions about good or beauty we can instead concentrate on more practical questions: how do things work and how might function serve form? Second, recent critical theory is a stirring reminder of our responsibility to history, our context, our culture and our specificity, ensuring that we work hard and not make lazy, offensive, solipsistic or thoughtless choices. Finally, problematising 'good' reminds us that our work—reading, making, judging—is always an assemblage, an act of assembly. It is not constructed after the fact from sub-headings such as plot, character, structure, theme and tone. It does not exist somewhere on an infinite incline from bad towards the eternally good. Judging by sub-heading and positioning on a scale happens after the work is made, and even then remains hotly contested.

Judging how the work is going as we make it, however, sees free play and *différance* as vital. Worrying about whether it is good as one is writing, fretting over sub-headings, wrestling with vague instructions like 'give it stakes' or 'more conflict' are generally non-starters. We must learn to read 'more gooderer'—how often do we stop and ask, as we are reading or writing, watching or witnessing:

What do I like? What stopped me or what did I want to know more of? What is working? How is this being achieved? What of the details, the gaps, the seeming contradictions? What of the brilliance, urgency, originality of a gesture, a word, a line, a relationship, a premise, a twist, a resolution? Likewise we must subject each atom of our writing to fission. Let us begin with the assumption that speaking and writing are always and already problems that we are in the midst of. Be responsible, be critical, re-think, agonise, plan, swap the bishop and the knight, cleave the general ear, let the misty rain fall.

If we worried only about the general good we would never make anything detailed, specific, sharp. When we developed Ian Wilding's *Quack* at Sydney's Griffin Theatre, we worried that using the zombie genre to tell a contemporary political story would be a hindrance, that it was fundamentally bad to use a popular film genre on the stage. Yet it delighted audiences, genre fans and critics. Genre allowed us to have a conversation with the audience before they arrived, with the pressure on us to add something entirely specific and new to the form. We paid close attention to the accord between structure, story increment and represented violence, excavating the various dramatic possibilities of shock.

Patricia Cornelius' muscular prose is reinvented with each of her plays, plays that are variously cruel, hilarious, wicked and written often as an intended affront to the good. Yet her work is lauded, winning her the prestigious Windham Campbell Award in 2019 on the strength of two antithetical plays, *Do Not Go Gentle* and *Shit*. Her plays mix register and diction, with almost every line, every gesture, rich with contradiction, rage and love. Restless, playful and unforgiving, Patricia stalks the good, kicking expected notions of taste in the guts and actively building plays that provoke, challenge and confound.

At every step of its development, the final scene of Aidan Fennessy's play *The Architect* was singled out as a bad idea. In it the main character chose assisted suicide to lingering death, a death we then witnessed—a truly shocking, and upsetting, *dénouement*. Yet it was the only play that I have ever worked on that was greeted, from first preview to closing night, with a standing ovation. A play about conviction, it held its line refusing to deviate from the logic of death; plus, in every moment it put a magnifying glass to the investigation of responsibility, as applicable to the makers as it is to the audience.

Each of these Australian playwrights collide the good with the bad, the tasteful with the ugly, the valuable with the worthless, leaving it to us to gather meaning, significance, utility. Indeed they utilise theatre's unique dynamic, the ability to toy with a live audience's expectations in real time. Just as a choice is made—at the level of metaphor and metonymy, character or plot—it is active, social and public. Here in the playing of the work itself we recognise worth, not in adherence to notions of supposed good but in the dissonance, the palpable friction, of actions, expectations, taste, folly and consequence, in the various shades, hues and shadows of good. The work itself functions at its best not because it observes the right path or is in itself virtuous, but because it compresses multiple value systems, letting audiences themselves argue over its goodness or otherwise.

If anything, it may be 'more gooderer' for us to worry less about the good than about performativity and language as it is used, contorted and abused; careful, detailed, pragmatic reading; and intimate, everyday uncertainty and its possibilities. Good, like plot, character or an actor's body, is most interesting when it is subjected to intense pressure—the job of any good play. Rather than good, be specific, detailed, fearless. Excavate and consider every verb you know. Share. Solicit. List. Chronicle events that have never happened so they never will. Just because the characters are evasive and fail to communicate, the theme is gnarly and the form jagged, the play may still be good. Is it urgent? Ambitious? Genuinely surprising? In this, some plays have tended to look a certain way, to follow similar structures, adopt an orthodoxy, but that does not in itself make them right or good. That is more due to certain lessons, orthodoxies, guide ropes, shortcuts, devices and contrivances. We will discuss them, and how plays look in the next *Thought*.

THOUGHT THREE

Structure: The magic number

One of my favourite glimpses into how stories work is by the American novelist and playwright Kurt Vonnegut. You can search for him and 'shape of stories' on the internet and there you will find grainy old colour video of a 1970s Vonnegut with chalk and a blackboard.[1] The lecture excerpt runs for less than five minutes. Apparently he had hoped to write a master's thesis in anthropology on his observations of shared story structures. Vonnegut considered that it would have brought scientific thinking—observation, hypothesis, testing, exactitude, iterability—to literary criticism, his 'prettiest' contribution to culture and certainly, for him, as revelatory as an ancient spearhead or pot.[2] He did not, however, write his thesis, just the proposal. The Anthropology Department of the University of Chicago rejected all his submissions, though much later credited him with an MA. Vonnegut was unimpressed by their rejection, but more so that no-one expressed gratitude for his bringing science, graphs and numbers to bear on the fuzzy and self-enclosed arts.

Vonnegut's proposal was to observe the significance of various central characters' emotional journeys and plot them on a graph. He drolly and drily runs through 'an exercise in relativity', remarking that it was 'the shape of the curve' that mattered. The x-axis measured Fortune—Good (at the top) and Ill (at the bottom)—with the horizontal y-axis running left to right from B to E, the story's Beginning to its End (as he is about to write E the audience starts laughing, and he quips that E stands for Electricity, or Entropy, depending on which version of the lecture you catch). It was a similar exercise to Freytag's representation of the best plays as pyramid-structured—though here stories are curves not straight lines.[3]

Vonnegut's overall hypothesis is a galvanising, unnerving and startling one: that there is a surprising commonality to most of our stories.[4] Vonnegut covers three story types as evidence of his hypothesis in the YouTube clip, giving each a distinctive name: Man in hole ('Somebody gets into trouble; gets out of it. People love that story!'); Boy gets girl (he comments that 'it needn't be that', describing it as 'somebody finds something wonderful, loses it, gets it back again'); and Cinderella (a character who starts out miserable, lower than average, has a taste of wonder, loses it, but is rewarded ultimately, when 'the shoe fits', with 'infinite happiness').

Vonnegut comments that none of these shapes are copyrighted, that you are welcome to use them and that every time someone does they make another million dollars. In a later version of this lecture, two more story types are included: Kafka's *Metamorphosis*, a plummeting curve to negative infinity; and *Hamlet* as a straight, flat line from beginning to end.[5] Amusingly, the more he goes on

THOUGHT THREE | STRUCTURE   37

to justify his argument about the analytical insights of the curves'
taxonomy, he seems to undermine it—his flattening of *Hamlet*
hinting that the ups and down do not really get to the heart of
literature at all. Literature's value rests—as Shakespeare's plays do—
in their telling of the truth, in compassion and empathy. Indeed
Vonnegut wryly observes that 'people so rarely tell the truth in this
rise and fall', too often pretending to know more than they actually
do.

Vonnegut here identifies two important things (his accusation
of literary arrogance and dissembling notwithstanding): that there
are elemental story structures in our culture; and that they can be
quantified—1. Man in hole, 2. Boy gets girl, 3. Cinderella, 4. Man turns
into cockroach, and 5. Flat *Hamlet*. Elsewhere Vonnegut, always
generous with advice, penned an idiosyncratic writing primer,
'Eight Rules for Writing'.[6] For a writer known to be whimsical, ironic
and digressive at best, his listing of eight rules and five story types
is both magnanimous and surprising. Vonnegut is far from alone,
however, in his point-by-point summaries. Nowadays guides and
writing manuals, especially dot-point and numbered abridgements
of key/essential/vital focal points, are ubiquitous. Irrespective of
their ubiquity, they raise fundamental questions: What is the best
way to assemble and analyse a story? Are there really just those few
to follow? Is there a magic number? Is it five?

In more recent guides, the number settled on seems to be seven.
Bestselling Australian author and Churchill Fellow Jen McVeity
achieved huge success, especially in Australian schools, with her
Seven Steps to Writing Success program. British journalist, author

and founder of satirical magazine *Private Eye* Christopher Booker wrote in 2004 of seven basic plots (overcoming the monster, rags to riches, the quest, voyage and return, comedy, tragedy and rebirth). American author and essay coach Alan Gelb also recommends seven steps to 'more confident writing', while Stanford Graduate School of business Professor Jennifer Aaker warns against the 'seven deadly sins of storytelling'.[7]

Type 'seven steps' into your search engine and you will be overwhelmed with numbered advice to increasing your genius, wealth, safety training, poetry reading skills and much more, with some going well beyond just seven steps: Pixar's 22 rules of storytelling; the twelve writing personalities (in the manner of Myers-Briggs); ten editing tips to becoming a better writer; the 20 master plots; story's 31 syntagmatic elements; 36 dramatic situations; ten ways to end your novel; ten steps to a winning plot; even character creation in seven steps with an accompanying software package for a monthly fee. Breaking tasks and stories into bite-sized pieces and manageable packets of phenomena is a widely accepted strategy, but how many pieces in a story and according to what?

My first contact with the practice of summarising stories into just a few numbered tropes and types (other than high school mnemonics) was not in English literature, or the popular press (I was raised well prior to BuzzFeed lists), but on a second year university course that straddled philosophy, English, linguistics, history and anthropology. There we read and discussed the development of semiotics and structuralism, reading Giambattista Vico, Ferdinand de Saussure, Claude Lévi-Strauss, Algirdas Julien Greimas, Tzvetan

THOUGHT THREE / STRUCTURE

Todorov, Edward Said, Ranajit Guha and Hayden White, among others. For me it was eye opening: the world inheres because of the relationship between things and according to their structural arrangement, not because of the things themselves. However, I was unsettled by the idea proposed in White's 1973 book *Metahistory* that

We need to be educated 'to discontinuity more than ever before; for discontinuity, disruption and chaos is our lot'

history (specifically, nineteenth-century history) could be reduced to four kinds of realist stories—romance, comedy, tragedy and satire, but also repudiated in three key ways, with metonymy, metaphor and irony. He maintained that historians were not scientists but storytellers. For White, history books were like any other, written by people who followed known literary structures in their plots. Narrative historians moulded discrete events into coherent stories, stories that were presented as meaningful histories, but which relied more on unacknowledged tropes than the facts. This was a radical re-configuring of the discipline of history. History, re-considered by White, was not false, but adhered to fictive arrangements dependent on historians' context, ideologies, beliefs and so forth. Critical of specious continuities, White instead urged that we needed to be educated 'to discontinuity more than ever before; for discontinuity, disruption and chaos is our lot'.[8] Chaos might be our lot, yet for him history could be reduced to four very orderly tropes.

Literary critic Northrop Frye was influential here. His 1957 *Anatomy of Criticism: Four Essays* called for critics to stand back from the close reading of texts and observe, scientifically, a certain 'archetypal organization' within and across them.[9] For Frye, all stories conformed to four key human myths, four myths like there are four seasons: comedy (spring), romance (summer), tragedy (autumn) and satire/irony (winter). He noted that there was a degree of variation in story types, hence suggesting six genre modifiers, ultimately offering a matrix of 24 *ur*-story types (*ur*, as a prefix, is from German, meaning 'out of' or even 'primitive', 'foundational', becoming widely adopted in English from the mid-twentieth century). Frye was plain that his four essays were incomplete but he also saw them as polemical, attempts at rethinking literary and cultural criticism using more than just words but allegory and archetype, ritual and dreams. He argued that the key to analysing story was to examine its structure and its impersonal, public nature in light of our Jungian collective unconscious.

If you are concerned that we started with five story types, expanded to seven then reverted to four, with a possible expansion to 24, we should briefly revise the work of Swiss psychoanalyst Carl Gustav Jung, as he was pivotal in popularising the notion of a limited number of shared, universal human types. He sought to create a typology of culture and maintained the existence of a non-deterministic and interactive relationship between culture and an individual's personality. Breaking with Freud just prior to World War I, Jung, initially in the late 1920s then in the late 1940s, postulated the existence of deep human instinctual patterns of behaviour and cognition evident in certain character 'archetypes'. He postulated that there were twelve of them, apparent in tribal lore, but also in fairytales and myths: ruler, creator/artist, sage, innocent, explorer, rebel, hero, wizard, jester, everyman, lover and caregiver. For Jung, myths were first and foremost psychic phenomena that revealed the unique nature and variety of the soul.[10]

Details of these archetypes have, for subsequent adherents, yielded a detailed organisational structure with which to excavate character (both real and fictional) as well as helping to explain the stories in which they are enmeshed. For instance, each human type had four distinctive core desires, a life goal and greatest fear, also idiosyncratic weaknesses and talents. Jung's work has had a problematic reception—his archetypes have been seen as vague, essentialist, reductive, racist, sexist and without rigour—within sociology, linguistics, anthropology and psychology (not to mention his possible anti-Semitism and Nazi collaboration) but the archetypes remain popular and persuasive.[11]

A simpler list seeking to explain all human behaviour, from a similar period, describes neither the corpus of world literature nor universal human types, just the five steps to human happiness. A foundational idea for Americans in particular, the pursuit of happiness can be linked to the Christian religion's belief in individual salvation but also to notions of public good and a fair and just society. Is happiness the highest good to which we can attain? Is happiness best measured by: how you feel now; how you lived your life; doing good in the world; one's social wellbeing, activism, occupation or even having voted? American psychologist Abraham Maslow ranked innate human needs, first in an article in 1943, then with a book in 1954. The path to happiness he catalogued was an easy-to-digest hierarchical list of five steps: first up were earthly needs, such as food (number one) and safety (two), essential because they acted as the groundwork for the pursuit of loftier needs and desires such as love or belonging (three), respect or esteem (four), and self-actualisation or the realisation of one's full potential (five), which he considered the apex of human goals.

As elegant as Maslow's five steps are, his theory was only ever that, a theory, and he has been critiqued for methodological problems (tiny sample size, fuzzy concepts, universal applicability). Two professors recently put it to the test, polling almost 61,000 participants across 123 countries, publishing the results in 2011.[12] They found that basic physiological needs were common across cultures. But they also found that needs were rarely simply either/or propositions, that they rarely occurred in as hierarchical a fashion as Maslow indicated (one could be happy with friends while also being hungry, for example), that the most common needs related to higher order requirements like love and esteem, and that needs were equally spread between lack of esteem, lack of freedom and lack of nourishment. Rather than a hierarchy, they found that for respondents balance was more important, with various needs all entangled and interrelated, indeed that individuals are happiest not only when their individual needs are being met but when their society as a whole is improving.

The search for a magic number that explains human action, cognition, and emotion, as well as the rudiments of story—that is, an elegant and straightforward way to reduce variability and complexity to structures that you can count on your hands, then enact—has proved challenging.[13] But there is the one theory, however, that abandons the idea of multiple underlying stories altogether, collapsing everything into one 'monomyth'. Joseph Campbell, a Jungian, wrote *The Hero with a Thousand Faces* in 1949 and while its impact in academe has been limited, it has been a colossal influence on popular culture. Critiqued after his death for his conservatism, naive romantic fascism and pan-spirituality, Campbell's work nevertheless indirectly structured some of the late twentieth century's most famous cultural artefacts, including the movies *2001: A Space Odyssey*, *Star Wars* and *Mad Max*.[14] Campbell believed that all hero stories essentially boiled down into the one *ur*-story, with the journey itself having multiple constituent parts—seventeen stages divided into three sections, or acts. Christopher Vogler simplified the journey to twelve steps in his hugely popular 1992 work, *The Writer's Journey*.[15] Any rough working knowledge of *Star Wars: A New Hope (Episode IV)* makes the schema plain.[16]

One myth, twelve parts, seven steps, five curves, four tropes: why all these numbered lists? Scientists now think that our brains enjoy easy reading, especially when the hard work of conceptualisation, categorisation and analysis has occurred prior to our consumption of the information. This is for four reasons. First, in a sea of words and images, numbers stand out.[17] Second, researchers recently discovered proof that we love an original headline but without too much actual new information.[18] Lists, and shortcuts to complex information, are intriguing enough to generate an immediate response, especially clicks, without requiring too much thinking from us. Third, our memories work better when information is condensed and put in a list, good for both quick understanding and effective recall.[19] Finally, with too much choice comes anxiety and confusion, but a list instead offers certainty and definite edges. They are also something we can finish, itself a pleasurable feeling.[20] Relying on lists means we sacrifice detail and nuance for efficiency of processing and for the pleasure of quick completion. Stepping through a task list, however, is clearly not the same as engaging with story, structure or language, symbol, metaphor or allegory. We like facts and logic, but we are built to understand things through story.[21]

One document that does both is the *Natya Shastra*, a Sanskrit treatise on the performing arts written sometime between 200 BCE and AD 200 and seemingly dictated to sage Bharata by Lord Brahma himself. Along with an almost infinite number of lists, the *Natya Shastra* offers extraordinary detail, nuance and complexity in a story. This holy Hindu text of approximately 6,000 poetic verses prescribes correct and appropriate performance modalities, including those for music, dance, playwriting and acting. For example, it allows for nine human emotions or 'rasas' (love, courage, surprise, loathing, terror, pity, disgust, anger and fun), ten types of play, two kinds of plot, five stages of action and five elements of plot, with specified numbers of junctures, sub-junctures, limbs, and so on. The first chapter makes it plain exactly what drama needs to do: represent the world, as it is now; describe how things work (duty, games, money, peace, laughter, love-making, fighting, killing, wisdom, sorrow, counsel, energy); and enlighten, divert and reward those who are ill-bred or unruly, cowardly or agitated, unlucky or afflicted, even wise and heroic. Drama should be, in essence, a 'happy adoration of the world'.[22]

The sheer number of lists contained in the *Natya Shastra*, their intersecting matrices, labyrinthine parts and directives hints perhaps at drama's sacred task, that is, for it to work it must capture some real world complexity. These lists, rather than being a mere distillation of the world, by their pure volume demand refinement, respect and multiplicity. Instead of trying to limit and contain, this compendium is a provocation to multiply, to liberate, to ask questions rather than follow strictures. Legendary director Anne Bogart, summarising the *Natya Shastra*, suggests that it is theatre itself that, in all its complexity, must pursue three tasks simultaneously: entertain the drunk; answer the question 'how to live?'; and answer the question, 'how does the universe work?'.[23]

Following the *Natya Shastra* and Anne Bogart, this direct list of three questions is an invocation, an entreaty, to let the content dictate the form, and to allow simple questions to drive complex answers, the answers of course being the work, the drama, itself. If I had asked emerging playwright Jean Tong about her divergence from the hero's journey, we would never have produced her shattering, radical and prismatic play *hungry ghosts*. If I had asked Gunditjmara playwright, poet, songwriter and elder Richard Frankland about adherence to story's seven steps, he would have patiently explained that such a regimented story was not his story; and such carelessness, arrogance, lack of respect and lack of listening on my part would never have seen us work successfully together on his groundbreaking plays *Conversations with the Dead* and *Walking into the Bigness*. If I had asked playwright Anchuli Felicia King about the four tropes of history, I expect she would have rigorously deconstructed the structuralist project altogether, and we would never have got to develop her formidable and subversive plays *Slaughterhouse* and *Golden Shield*. Each of these Australian plays took huge risks with form and structure, with storytelling tropes and with presumptions of character.

It is a mantra amongst dramaturgs to be sure to ask the right questions (in fact it is dramaturgy's fundamental modality, but we will circle back to that in a while), but with the wrong questions, with enforced structures, with inflexibility or too much certainty, or worse, righteousness, we can de-centre a scene, discombobulate a character, eviscerate a play, and marginalise or silence a playwright, forever locking the work in an *oubliette*, echo chamber or bottom drawer. Plays are built as a creative and intersecting series of provocations, not just to follow—nor are they themselves—a list of instructions.

There is no answer to the question of how a play's form and content should match but it is our sacred task to fulfil it. There are no easy seven steps, no useful theatre Lego or Ikea instruction sheet, doll's house or train track—though there are loads of how-to guides claiming otherwise. That lack of instruction manual, that invocation to match content with form, is at the heart of the

THOUGHT THREE / STRUCTURE   47

scepticism, anxiety and joy of creating theatre, something we simultaneously do from scratch while also entirely from within our own culture/s. Each writer discovers it their way, and most importantly the discovery itself reveals that our task is not linear, that theatre may even be non-Euclidean (that is, elliptic, hyperbolic, obtuse, 3D, curved, maybe poly-dimensional).

It does help though to clarify a play's public and private timelines and to imagine real options considering open and closed time and space. It also helps to consider playwright and director David Lan's provocation that each play only contains five steps.[24] The tasks ahead of us include pain and joy—indeed that is playwriting's promise— and to expect, to seek out and be inspired by research, context and time, memory, resistance and terror, myth, science and curiosity, certainty and uncertainty, good humour, ethics, patience and care, injustice, rage and risk, fear and desire, thrills, spells, delicacy, impact, caution, contradiction, slowness, bodies, hospitality, and much else besides. It is hard work. Is there a structure for this?

Suzan Lori-Parks speaks to this in her stunning *Elements of Style*— in fact her first imperative is the interdependence of form and content—in which she talks about the importance of repetition and revision, etymology and history, things that keep her awake, but also about 'math' and 'bad math'.[25] In the 'math' section she draws impossible, ironic diagrams that are her demonstrations of the 'equations of some plays'. In each of the diagrams she includes the phrase (itself a provocation about numbered lists, gender and race bias and plays unfolding along a two dimensional line), 'Solve for X' and 'Solve for X where X is the true measurement of the Great Man's

Stature' (X, in maths, is commonly understood to be the stand-in for an unknown value). In the margin there is also a note, titled 'Pickling' (to preserve the shelf life of a play?) in which she reiterates that the 'play is trying to find an equation for time *saved*/saving time' but that 'theatre/experience/performing/being/living' is actually all about 'spending time', making the equation unworkable. For her, plays are about accumulation, language, humour, history and action, not lists and hierarchies, and they involve 'your whole bod'. In 'bad math' she warns against plays as 'merely staged essays' in which characters are symbols for some deferred, 'obscured "meaning"'. She implores the reader: 'Don't ask playwrights what their plays mean; rather, tell them what you think and have an exchange of ideas.' Theatre, here, is not about adhering to lists or two-dimensional lines, but about digging, finding, writing 'with your whole bod', reading 'with your whole bod'; that, and to 'Wake up'.

Oh but—surprise!—there is a magic story number, and in 2016 computer scientists proved it: six.[26]

Thought Four
Character: The source, the principle, the foundation and the guide

As a high school student I wrote grindingly dull essays about ye olde plays, formulaically responding to staggering characters and fierce dramatic works with weak insights and a rote assessment of the plight of the relevant tragic hero. Yet 'hero', I now know, is a word with a specific meaning in ancient Greece, a demi-god (someone half human, half immortal), and was used only later by the Romans to mean an illustrious, noble person, a courageous warrior and model citizen. It entered English in the seventeenth century in the same lion-hearted vein, and from the Restoration onwards was also used to denote the principal character in a play.

When thinking about plays it is not uncommon to conflate a play with its main character. A character is self-evidently not the same as a play but given that so many pre-twentieth century plays are named after their eponymous protagonists—*Medea*, *Antigone*, *Hamlet*, *Helen*, *Edward II*, *King Lear*, *Andromache*, even *The Rover*, and so many more—it is certainly an easy way to remember the play, while also being attractive to actors (title role!) and audiences (great actor plays title role!). Yet just when the protagonist and the hero had begun to become synonymous, the hero began to morph.

Once purely descriptive of a regal central character with external goals, a formal imperative and significant story obstacles, by the late eighteenth century 'hero' had begun to signify a character beset by a brooding, rocky emotional landscape—family problems, imminent war or a city at the mercy of the Sphinx were no longer enough. The Romantic literary period is not always beloved by scholars for its contribution to theatre repertoire[1]—with some of Shakespeare's plays even re-written to better fit the times[2]—but piteous, forlorn and glorious characters, heroes and heroines hell-bent on achieving impossible goals while 'smothering her sufferings in the deepest recesses of her own wretched bosom ... writhing thus under her internal agonies', became a staple of the popular stage from the late eighteenth century.[3] Foregrounded here are not plot or a moral lesson, but character, emotion, passion and the heartache hidden deep inside the hero or heroine.

Classical character templates were, in this light, sidelined as artificial, staid and formal. In place of questions of ethos, meter or the Three Unities, sobriety, valour or uprightness, the focus shifted to self-expression and personal torment. A play's protagonist, the hero, here became Byronic, a reckless, sensitive, defiant, self-aware freedom fighter chasing grand, incessant passions, rejecting all conventions and abandoning rational standards of conduct.[4] These incendiary warriors against tyranny and tormented princelings delighted and terrified audiences, as well as delighting and terrifying the actors who played the windswept and unruly roles. Character, in particular individual subjectivity and the hero's 'hidden abysses', as Romantic essayist, critic, philosopher and poet A.W. Schlegel coined it, moved to centre-stage.[5] The external dramatic world was subordinated to the internal, the former often merely a synecdoche for the latter.

We live in the shadow of these two important shifts—an exceptional focus on character and a character's interior world, and a developing understanding of character itself as more than a God-given entity but as a site of torment, competing imperatives and painful emotional mysteries. For Aristotle the protagonist had a job to do and emotion was important insofar as the audience experienced catharsis. Here, however, characters and their emotions became the key to unlocking a play. Tennessee Williams, idealist and romantic, whose plays are famous for their striking, often doomed, certainly covertly tormented characters—Blanche, Stanley and Stella, Brick, Maggie and Big Daddy, Amanda, Tom and Laura—wrote in 1955:

> My characters make my play. I always start with them, they take spirit and body in my mind. Nothing they say or do is arbitrary or invented. They build the play about them like spiders weaving their webs, sea creatures making their shells … I know them far better than I know myself, since I created them and not myself.[6]

Do characters and their internal, barely understood but deeply felt, emotional turbulence write their own plays as Williams suggested?

In writing a play, the playwright wrestles with the play's world, tone, imagery, diction and register, structure, ongoing inspiration, plot mechanics, heartache and the thousand natural shocks that flesh is heir to, with character just one among multiple tools, textures, threads, lines of flight. Indeed many playwrights and theatre makers, certainly irregularly so from the 1890s, rejected 'character as hero' and the expectation that the empathic and anguished heart of the play, its gravitational centre, was the hero's journey. Their plays questioned, de-centred and deconstructed such a dramatic fiction—think, in particular, of the work of Maurice Maeterlinck, Luigi Pirandello, Bertolt Brecht or Samuel Beckett. In some recent plays of the British playwright Martin Crimp for instance, Aristotle was even taken at his word—that plays can exist without characters but not without plot—with plays written entirely without a single character being named or designated. Yet a great character, like a brilliant actor, sells tickets.

Indeed when workshopping new plays, a perennial, stealthy, silent judgement hovers over the question of character, particularly if there is a producer in the room ready to venture their thoughts: not only whether the hero's emotional plight is relatable, but is the hero and their predicament believable and are they likeable? Indeed, the more familiar the hero's struggle, the more likely actors are to become emboldened and offer their view on the veracity or otherwise of a particular line of dialogue or course of action.

But is a play a popularity contest and should its characters follow expected paths? Do we like Hamlet? Would we make Antigone's choices? Is a complex work of dramatic art just a reflection of the central character's psyche? Such simplistic rendering of a play's multiplicity, however, does hint at a particular fuzziness, a blurriness when it comes to the making, playing and interpreting of theatre, and that is the supplanting of dramatic action and plot by character and emotion. As we have mentioned, character and play are, more often than not, inextricably interlinked by playwrights, actors and audiences. Is this blurring entirely the fault of the Romantics? This near synonymity of Romantic hero and play also points us to a phenomenon that is entirely recent, yet, strangely, one that feels like a veritable and ancient precept: the interdependence of plays and psychology. That is, to know the play, to really know it, we need to plumb the character's depths, and to do that we must utilise psychology.

Given that psychology became a discipline around 1890 (William James wrote *The Principles of Psychology* in 1890 and the year before the International Congress of Psychology met for the first time in Paris) yet drama in its recognised form dates from roughly 2,500 years ago, theatre, plays and performance had, for a very long time, seemingly done fine without it. Psychology has nevertheless quickly come to influence conversations and, more importantly, explanations of plays, their insights and their practical realisation. In Aristotle's hierarchy, plot preceded character, yet over the course of the twentieth century in particular, 'character' as an organising principle, emotional guide and analytical tool has come to command all before it. Theories of drama, whether from Aristotle or Freytag, began to pale in the face of a new science— accurate, built on hard evidence and manifestly true. Constructed slowly over 200-plus years by myriad theorists and experimentalists (the seventeenth century saw Gottfried Leibniz postulating a kind of mental calculus while Qing Dynasty thinkers theorised the nervous system, with the word itself coined in 1732), the science of emotion could now explain the raw, Romantic heart of the dramatic arts, the mysteries of hidden, or worse, caged emotions.

That psychology is invoked when new plays are being workshopped is a truism, an inevitability. What of the character's journey? Do we believe each moment? Their backstory? Is it likely, accurate and complete? Yet, how would we know? In order to anticipate the sometimes premature turn to psychology when analysing a play, legendary dramaturg and scholar Elinor Fuchs wrote the groundbreaking essay 'EF's Visit to a Small Planet' and peppered it with questions to impede character-based bias. She wrote that the 'questions' were 'in part designed to forestall the immediate (and crippling) leap to character and normative psychology that underwrites much dramatic criticism'.[7]

Is psychology 'crippling' when it comes to playwriting and analysis or does it unlock and deepen writing, performance and a play's reception? Many of us freely discuss 'character', yet few of us are qualified psychologists or psychiatrists, psychoanalysts or psychotherapists, so how did we become such experts in it? And, how did 'character', and its analytical archipelago, become the key bearer, sometimes sole arbiter, of a play's secrets, and its success?

Perhaps it all started with Psyche. If you don't know her myth, it is a hell of a story—though of course merely one in a teeming throng of ancient Greek tales of betrayal, vengeance, ferocity, compassion, happenstance, metamorphoses and occasional tendernesses. Sometimes seen as the source myth of *Beauty and the Beast* and

Cinderella, it involves a beautiful mortal woman, Psyche, subject to the rage of the goddess of love, Aphrodite, jealous because locals have started worshipping Psyche's beauty. To appease the gods, Psyche's dad leaves her on a rock to be taken by a sea monster, but because of her beauty she is instead rescued by Aphrodite's son Cupid.[8] He whisks Psyche off to his castle and all proceeds with joy—though he does insist that they only spend time together at night in the dark. Psyche knows it is a little weird but her jealous sisters convince her to sneak an oil lamp in when he's sleeping—he might be a hideous monster—and she is transfixed by his beauty. Unfortunately, dripping hot oil wakes him and he abandons her. Aphrodite then sets Psyche four trials, each of which she succeeds in but she collapses while completing the final task (it involves going to the Underworld to secure a secret of Persephone's, which Psyche accomplishes, but, when curiosity gets the better of her, Psyche looks at the secret and falls into a torpor). Cupid saves her and brings her up to Olympus where Zeus makes her immortal and the Goddess of the Soul. Psyche had fallen pregnant in Cupid's castle (unbeknownst to Cupid) and on Olympus she gives birth to their child, Hedone (Pleasure).

Is it an allegory, a fable, a parable? Is meaning hidden below the surface, or is the surface dense enough just as it is?

Need a quick recap? Psyche experiences beauty, worship, jealousy, abandonment, love, deception, torment, subterfuge, abandonment (again), humiliating and exhausting trials, actual hell, success, paralysis, love (again), elevation to a god, childbirth, and a child who is literally pleasure. Is it an allegory, a fable, a parable? Is meaning hidden below the story's surface, or is the surface dense enough just as it is?[9]

The descriptive term itself, psyche, was also adopted into philosophy and medicine. This is because in Greek the word means life, a vital breath, spirit, consciousness, or soul. It became a contested philosophical idea with Plato and Socrates having quite a different view to Aristotle's. For Plato and Socrates the soul, psyche, was immortal and separate from the body. Aristotle held, however, that it was tripartite (vegetable, animal and rational human) and could not be separated from the body; indeed the soul gave the body life, reason, truth and true purpose. The soul, for Aristotle, imprinted on the body as a wax seal does on wax, with the impression no different to the wax itself. He ranked study of the soul, in his book *De Anima* (*On the Soul*), as being not just about 'noble and estimable things' as with other knowledge, but about 'better and more wondrous things', for psyche was the starting point of all living things. Contributing as much to biology as to psychology, philosophy and theology, he saw psyche as the universal essence of being. Aristotle looked to study the ways that being was effected and whether the soul (psyche or anima) was a thing of substance and form, or a quality, and whether it/they are one, universally, or differ across genus or species.

The developing medical profession began to adopt the prefix 'psych' along with 'logia' when the 'study of the soul' was picked up by European Renaissance and Enlightenment philosophers, theologians and proto-scientists, from Thomas Aquinas to Immanuel Kant, from Petrus Ramus and Juan Luis Vives to Francis Bacon,

René Descartes and John Locke, all of them seeking to comprehend virtue, sensation, mental experience and its manifestation in action and behaviour. One of the first extant works with the actual term in its optimistic title was Rudolph Goclenius' 1590 *Psychology, or the perfection of man, his mind and its origin* (*Psychologia: de hoc est hominis perfectione, animo, et in primis*). While more theological and ontological than what we would understand as psychological, Goclenius was most certainly bullish about the discipline's potential. Indeed an eighteenth-century Swiss encyclopedia entry from almost 200 years later was just as hopeful:

> ... without knowledge of the nature, faculties, qualities, state, relations and destination of the human soul, we can pass judgment on nothing, decide nothing, determine nothing, choose nothing, reject nothing, prefer nothing and do nothing with certainty and without error. Psychology is consequently the first and most useful of all the sciences, the source, the principle and the foundation of them all, as well as the guide which leads to each.[10]

The encyclopedia was published in 1774, so such bravura was very early, given that psychology had yet to formally coalesce into an institutional scholarly pursuit or offer any hard evidence that human perfectibility could even be realised through its ministrations.

Beyond the distinct philosophical traditions of metaphysics, logic, morality and ontology, beyond axioms and suppositions on the anatomy of the soul, so there grew another mode of inquiry, initially evident in Vives' insistence on observation, experiment and measurement, Charles Bell's surgical operations on the brains of wounded soldiers, Christian Wolff's 'apperceptions', Ernst Weber's analysis of physical stimuli, Jean Pierre Flourens' or Claude Bernard's vivisections, William Tuke and Esther Maud's 'moral management', or Gustav Fechner's 'psychophysics'. This other tradition, more empirical than scholastic, focused not just on the soul but on the mechanics of sensation, passion and the imagination, on how the human mind grew and developed, how it acted and reacted to its environment, how intelligence, memory and character were formed, and how nerves actually worked. Voltaire, in his entry to the French Encyclopedia on 'soul', had wondered: 'What a fine thing it would be to see one's soul'.[11] This practical study of the mind sought to do just that, and it slowly became a new discipline, experimental psychology, that reached its apotheosis in Wilhelm Wundt's Leipzig laboratory in 1879, or perhaps in Freudians scribing the first two editions of the extremely influential *Diagnostic and Statistical Manual of Mental Disorders* (the manuals of 1952 and 1968), the key reference work used by clinicians, researchers, regulatory agencies, health insurance and pharmaceutical companies, the legal system, and policy makers in the mid-twentieth century.

We will come back to Wundt and Freud, and the development of the lab for the mind momentarily, but before we do, it is worth noting that just as psyche had two distinct but related meanings, so it is with character.[12] It might seem self-evident and rather bleedingly obvious that character relates not just to fictional creations but also to real people's behaviours, yet so often our analysis of one blurs into the other, and vice versa, as if they were the same. Part of the trick of theatre, its spell or special cognitive *jouissance*, is that we imagine ourselves into the character that is, for many, the empathetic heart of theatre. As a result, the fiction becomes real—we will have a look at this later—and we not only expect a fictional character's behaviour to be credible but authentic, at least in our subjective experience of what 'authentic' might be, otherwise the spell is broken and the play fails to engage. As psychology itself grew and developed, so certain words, tools and concepts entered popular discourse and the deciphering of character, real and fictional, for an explanatory pathology became commonplace. Yet fictional characters are not real and plays are rarely documentaries, with characters rarely if ever played by the real people on stage. Beyond that, with no training in psychology, we are nevertheless confident to lean on its authority and parrot some of its lexicon. What are we thinking?

The late twentieth and early twenty-first centuries have seen us steeped in psychology.[13] Maybe, firstly, it is because some of the most memorable mythological figures—Oedipus, Electra, Narcissus, Priapus, the Furies, Phobos and so on—are also some of the most famous psychological terms and disorders, blurring the line between psychological truth and imaginative writing. As to writing itself, bookshop shelves are crowded with self-help companions and pop psychology treatises. Turn on a television at prime time and the dominant form, reality TV, depicts 'real' contestants, but only as the embodiment of archetypical stories—the hero, the villain, the sage, the jester and so forth—and as expressed in their 'journeys', for instance how they overcame personal demons to learn to love/work/cook again. Here in 'reality' or 'unscripted' drama, personal suffering and mental health challenges are commodified as entertainment. Expert terms, conditions and complexes are also quoted well outside medical environments with no real expertise or research—inner child, CBT, self-esteem, emotional intelligence, archetype and so on. As a result, mere mention of a cigar, a couch, Dr Phil, Dr Spock, Dr Jekyll, Prozac, the id, the Skinner Box, body language or even mother, elicit immediate responses. British clinical psychologist Stephen Briers asserted recently that:

> The ideas and values associated with popular psychology have infiltrated our culture so deeply that we now take them largely for granted. Even for those of us who regard ourselves as fairly knowing, they form part of that framework of assumptions that constitutes the invisible scaffolding for the way we approach our lives.[14]

As a result, being in rehearsal, or just being in the world, means that when reading a play or analysing a character, discussing friends, family or colleagues, trying to parent or solving everyday human problems, we can fall back on what we hope is psychology, but is just as likely to be pseudo-science, urban myth, self-help or superstition. And for us in the theatre, this is doubly complicated by the coincident birth of psychology with modern acting theory.

Wundt, later Freud and many, many other experimental psychologists and psychiatrists, contributed to the development of a new technology in the eighteenth and nineteenth centuries. Wundt, as with another German researcher, Gustav Fechner, took the study of the mind out of the hospital and into the laboratory, the home of physicists and chemists, temples to accuracy, objectivity and safety. In a laboratory the object of analysis, in this case the patient (animal or human), could be isolated then probed, tested, examined, discussed, analysed, written-up and classified. Wundt sought to determine the basic elements of thought, to comprehend how they connected and then observe the laws by which mental elements combined to become mental experiences. Theories of the relationship between the mind and the body, behaviour and phenomena, were tested in his laboratory in two discrete ways: first, through experiments on patients to measure the basic nerve processes; and then through observation, introspection and assessment for the higher mental processes.

These new techniques—experimentation, measurement, introspection, and observation—were emulated in similar laboratories set up by like-minded researchers in other German cities. Students flocked to Wundt's Leipzig lab in extraordinary numbers—Wundt personally supervised 186 doctoral theses and it was reported that 'there was no lecture room in the university large enough' for his classes. From 1879 those students then set up their own labs and experimental laboratory practices in their cities of origin. These diagnostic institutional models (the separate research laboratory) were then replicated across Europe, North and South America (initially at the influential Harvard and Cornell universities), India, China, Egypt, Japan and Australia over the following 20 years.[15]

Despite medicine's heterogeneous contest of ideas, as a disciplinary practice the psychological sciences agreed on three fundamentals: first, that medical doctors brought unprejudiced truths to light through the experimentation on, and description and examination of, human bodies; second, that knowledge acquired through observing and analysing human behaviour (and recorded into written discourse for further analysis and posterity) was to better manage patients' physical and psychological maladies; and finally, that this new technical act of observing, notating and classifying people psychologically united medicine, biology and philosophy.[16] As intellectual historian Michel Foucault has argued, the 'turning of real lives into writing' was no longer 'a procedure of heroization' but instead, in the new medical institutional complex, it functioned as 'a procedure of objectification and subjectification'.[17]

Nineteenth-century medicine and its various studies of humans in clinics, labs and asylums created an entirely new way to look at humanity, that is, with a certain penetrating, diagnostic gaze. People could be calibrated, interpreted and explained just by looking at them, their hidden, secret, as-yet-unknown predilections, lesions and pathologies, if viewed with a critical, clinically trained eye. This gaze privileged the doctor's learned and technical view over and above the patient's experience, symptoms or voice—though psychology and psychiatry would soon encourage those vocal utterances to play their part in the medicalisation of the docile patient's body and mind.[18] Human attributes and deficiencies could be better understood with respect to their conformity to, or deviation from, certain discernible behavioural norms and habits.[19] Observation of conduct, habits and manners allowed medical experts to assess individuals' capacities and demeanour in order to determine where their patients could best be managed, utilised and deployed—indeed psychologists learnt to perform 'an "autopsy" of the living'.[20] If judged feeble-minded, delinquent or a pauper, for instance, a patient might be better institutionalised and cared for under regular watchful medical instruction.

Newly discovered psychological truths also offered opportunities for the therapeutic remodelling of our lives, with life itself a project of gradual psychic fulfilment, dependent upon the normative operation of medical expertise and training in behavioural techniques that themselves also taught a new art of decoding habit, conduct and manners. As one scholar has argued: 'It is increasingly to psychologists that the citizens ... look when they seek to comprehend and surmount the problems that beset the human condition—despair, loss, tragedy, conflict—living their lives according to a psychological ethic.'[21] Indeed, as philosopher Paul Ricoeur has argued, a new hermeneutic enterprise is required of us, that is, that meaning must be mapped onto meaning.[22] Symptoms of neuroses (hysteria or the content of dreams, for instance) in everyday behaviour represent a superficial level of meaning, a distorted level of imagination, gesture, feeling and language, with a new and deeper level of meaning remaining to be uncovered, brought to light only through the doctor's understanding of their patient. It was a relationship that Freud honed away from a hospital, away even from a lab, in the doctor's private rooms.

This persuasive new scientific mode of uncovering and mapping character—of observing, notating and discussing temperament, behavioural habits and the outward manifestations of inner turmoil, of inscribing and recording psychic attributes and deficiencies, of searching for truth and of rendering the real—would soon be taken up in the theatre. For some Freudians, characters even developed prior to language, and certainly prior to and independent of the plays in which they appeared (and who else but Freudians would find significance in lists of *dramatis personae* appearing *prior* to speeches they are yet to deliver?), speaking with a language that reflects their experiential and psychological history, characters only extant as effects of language itself. The role of the doctor was soon to be played by the new and emergent force in the rehearsal room, the director. As it had in wider culture, the discussion of character would literally move to centre-stage, de-centring the discussion of other aspects of performance. Theatre itself, however, had yet to change in some fundamental ways.

Theatre scholar Joseph Roach has observed that acting theories changed over time, themselves closely reflecting society's prevailing scientific and medical beliefs through history. And in that, the nineteenth and early twentieth centuries are no different. In the late nineteenth century the nature of theatrical rehearsal

The role of the doctor was soon to be played by the new and emergent force in the rehearsal room, the director

began to lengthen, thanks in large part to the Duke of Saxe-Meiningen's colossal shows (and complicated touring schedules) requiring multiple weeks, sometimes months, of rehearsal, and theatre managements began to cram in up to 4,000 seats in enormous theatres. In response, actors (such as Mikhail Shchepkin, Gustavo Modena, Tommaso Salvini, Adelaide Ristori, Lyubov Nikulina-Kositskaya, Mademoiselle Rachel [Elisabeth-Rachel Félix], Edwin

Booth, Ernesto Rossi and Eleonora Duse) and acting companies (such as under Madame Vestris, Marie Wilton and Squire Bancroft, Montigny or the Parisian Théâtre-Libre) sought solace from the huge crowds and stock gestures in tiny theatres, using real props and real tears. When European writers, fired by the squalor, injustice and poverty of late nineteenth-century cities, sought redress through literature, theatre's stories, architecture, stage properties, blocking and notions of actor preparation all began to shift.

French novelist and pamphleteer Émile Zola even called for the 'gradual substitution of physiological man for metaphysical man'.[23] He demanded to know what plays might be like if life was staged as it actually was. What of the poor, the working class, the disenfranchised, the uneducated? What of the insights of scientific analysis, biological determinism and 'the frightening lesson of sincere investigation ... the anatomy of man ... in an exact reproduction, more original and powerful than anyone has so far dared to risk on the boards'?[24] For Zola, theatre must no longer lie by imposing an ornamental, classical or Romantic formula on the world, but itself be reactive, invisible, observant, curious, returning to 'simplicity of action' and 'unique psychological and physiological study of character' in order to 'increase the reality of the corpus of our drama, to progress towards truth, to sift out more and more of the natural human'.[25]

In the late nineteenth century, a wealthy, very tall amateur Russian actor heeded the call for scientific character realism, though his response owed more to Shchepkin's legacy, the Meinengen Ensemble's sets and longer rehearsals, and his own perceived acting failures than to Zola's essay. Drama school dropout

Konstantin Sergeyevich Stanislavsky agonised over making acting more real, doing so over a very slow, almost 30-year journey towards wanting to liberate performers from tics and tired contrivances. In his sights were the exaggerated movements required in very large theatres, the clichés of conventional routines and blind eyes to performer's laziness, fear, idiosyncrasies and indulgences. Instead he sought to develop a deeper, more considered method of actor training, embracing longer rehearsals and current scientific thinking about reflexes, behaviour and emotions and let them be his guide. Writing in his memoir, and considering his own weak acting choices as a young man in the 1880s, he figured the only option for better acting was pseudo-medical, an operation: 'an amputation, a disembowelling, a draining of the theatrical muck that still remained secretly hidden'.[26] Later, after a crisis of confidence in 1907, he gathered his now famous acting company together and tried to overcome Denis Diderot's paradox of the actor (deliberation versus unrestrained impulse) with what was then cutting-edge technology—the psychological experiments of Théodule-Armand Ribot and Ivan Pavlov: 'I tortured them [the actors]; they grew angry and said that I had turned rehearsals into an experimental laboratory, and that actors were not guinea pigs to be used for experimentation.'[27] It is a common misconception that Stanislavsky ever read Freud; he did not. To solve the actor's conundrum of repeating 'real' emotion, Stanislavsky was convinced the answer lay in science and psychological laws: 'Such laws exist for all, for ever and in all creative processes ... tried by science and found true, and binding on all. Each actor must know them.'[28]

THOUGHT FOUR / CHARACTER

Perhaps Stanislavsky's greatest contribution, however, was to the institution of acting itself, literally. His continued calls for the profession to 'become habit', for actors to submit to a regimen, that is, to continuous training, to a 'system', and for it to become second nature through years of training, became enshrined in the institution of the modern repertory acting school. It was here in acting schools that the restlessness of his 'system' could meet the requirements necessary for truthful acting, the perfect harmony of physique and will, conscious and super-conscious emotions, hard physical effort and inner spiritual challenges, premeditation and spontaneity: all through the psychologist's methodology of introspection, observation, repetition, time and patience in a training laboratory/conservatory. This movement would reach its zenith with the establishment of the American Academy of Dramatic Arts in 1884 in New York City, the Royal Academy of Dramatic Arts in 1904 and the Central School of Speech Training and Dramatic Art in 1906 (now Central School of Speech and Drama), both in London, buildings in which to devote time and patience to the balance between mind, body, intention, truth and the audience.[29] While Stanislavsky's system itself was restless, often misunderstood and continues to be translated and unpacked, the institutions devoted to making normative behaviour second nature were perhaps his most substantial physical, literal legacy. Built from bricks and mortar, Stanislavsky's system has bequeathed generation after generation of actors with the idea that learnt, embodied, articulate psychology is central to the theatrical process.

That there are problems and contradictions with psychology,

and character, in play analysis or the play development workshop or rehearsal room is evident in a number of ways. First, what of context and anachronism? That is, how relevant is psychology to a play written before it existed? Second, should rehearsal take, or even have, the time required to fully excavate, diagnose and treat both the real and fictional characters present? Does therapy ever end? And should it be rehearsed by the unqualified? Third, if character is just one mask of many, is there a limit to the masks we wear, to the institutional, political and social rules dictating norms and behaviours, and to the irreconcilable problems of self-scrutiny? Indeed, is character just one more disorder among many? Who is the arbiter when it comes to 'normal' or 'correct' behaviour, bullying and harassment notwithstanding? Finally, perhaps it is worth recalling postdramatic theatre, its suspicion of character and the privileging of humanist discourse, most especially its pursuit of a character's 'real' inner life. In light of the performance paradigms of Antonin Artaud and Jerzy Grotowski, the actor is but a body moving through a space, part of an accepted ritual of dynamic accretions. Here actors are less motivated by representation, fractured psyches or embodied pathologies than liberated by theatrical possibilities, with characters' limited strictures abandoned altogether.

When it comes to writing a play, it is of course not uncommon to start with a character, a phrase uttered by someone or an image of a person in a particular, often difficult, place. Is character so unstable as a concept, however, that this is to be avoided? If we develop a hunch or an inkling about someone imagined, and their suffering, is it to be shunned? Not at all. In Paul Livingston's play *Emma's Nose* for instance, a play literally about Freud and his character, Livingston displayed little interest in any of the characters' psychological depths. Wickedly silly, it did, however, have a lot to say about the curious birth of psychoanalysis, its blindnesses, damage and legacy. In Damien Millar's searing portrait of Australian international aid workers, *The Modern International Dead*, while the characters' psychic trauma was front and centre (though they would never have expressed or even seen it that way), we watched just three actors play more than 30 characters between them, one a real person, one a composite of two real people, and one a medley of multiple real people. Any desire to plumb their individual depths, explore their unique trauma, or psychoanalyse their motives would upset every other scene as each of the three central characters' subjectivity was flipped and flipped again as the three actors played their multiple roles. The play did not spare details of global politics, the internecine struggles of the military or the sometime hypocrisy of aid work, and, despite no single protagonist, empathy still occurred, with the play being enjoyed across multiple productions. The character 'Lally Katz' usually appears in real playwright Lally Katz's plays: evidence of a psychic disturbance, overweening narcissism or an old trick, misdirection? Or even worse perhaps, a sly way of including exposition via direct narration? Or did 'Lally Katz' enable the plays to ask other, more troubling, questions about representation, expectation and narrative closure? And in the two co-written plays of Andrew Bovell, Patricia Cornelius, Melissa Reeves, Christos Tsiolkas and Irine Vela, *Who's Afraid of the Working Class?* and *Anthem*, with their avowed aim of theatrical class, race and gender analysis, à la Bertolt Brecht's *gestus* in Epic Theatre, character is just one of many theatrical tools at the disposal of the actors, creative team and the audience, with character psychology both fundamental for making the familiar strange and the strange familiar, but also, a bourgeois trap.

From the late eighteenth century, as the protagonist became the hero, the play text was re-mapped to reveal a new kind of imagined *ur*-writing, subtext, so character became not simply descriptive of a job but an embodied diagnosis, psychic refuge, hidden enclave, psychological network and egoist edifice. In Heiner Müller's play *Mauser* (1970), itself an over-writing of Brecht's learning/teaching play *The Measures Taken* (1930), character 'A' claims, 'I am a human' but the Control Chorus replies, 'What is that', both accusation and question. While Brecht had rejected humanism as a bourgeois error, Müller's play is a dense and dramatic wrestle with simplistic assumptions and easy certainties, humanist or ideological. 'A' is on trial in both plays, having made mostly well-intentioned mistakes, and as a result the Control Chorus informs 'A' to agree to their own execution: 'For your hand is not your hand ... For what is natural is not natural.' The future demanded it, history had spoken over A's assumption as to the innate and self-evident value of humanity. Character, and our analytical use of it, too often settles on certainty when it is in fact a rarely examined fault line, a fault zone, indeed a cluster of fault traces—action at the mercy of words, behaviours and concepts already under stress: identity, naturalness, spontaneity, premeditation, human rights, necessity, freedom. Character is explanatory only insofar as it relies on words, behaviours and concepts that exist at the edge of a certain metaphysical surplus. Rather than accepting normative behaviours, we must learn to embrace 'character' as stress, contradiction and opportunity. Such fault lines, zones and traces are the places of drama, thresholds of friction, dissonance and ingenuity. As Müller's Chorus warns/ counsels/obfuscates/annihilates/declaims: 'That it must be done here today / So that it must be done no longer and by no-one.'

THOUGHT FIVE

Dramaturgy: An ample margin

Discussing medical matters, as we were in the previous *Thought*, reminds me of being in the UK on a bursary in 1998 and raising the topic of dramaturgy with a number of the UK's then artistic directors and literary managers. The word was received with a measure of scepticism, disdain and repugnance. One artistic director even laughed at my use of the word, commenting on their aversion to 'that German virus'.

I was a quite taken aback. First, dramaturgy as a pathogen neither dead nor alive that replicates inside the cells of host organisms—ultimately killing them—seemed rather an extreme comparison, both as to dramaturgy's efficiency and its destructive capacity. Second, were we not all in this together? That is, should we not do all we could, employ all the tools in our arsenal no matter their provenance, to see the finest work make it to our stages? Finally, dramaturgy was German? Not having studied theatre (but English literature and Australian history) I had heard it spoken of and figured that it was something ancient, probably Greek, that we in Australia had synthesised (like so much else at that time) from European and American theatres where it was considered commonplace, not controversial. Still, in some remote corner of my mind was the memory that both Bertolt Brecht and Heiner Müller were dramaturgs, and playwrights, and German.

On returning to Australia and reviewing the literature at the time, most prolific in the US, dramaturgy was indeed slowly moving from out of the margins. It was a practice performed by dramaturgs, it was also known as being a 'script doctor' or 'play midwife'. The job, and the position, was performed by someone trained in research, drama's rules and customs but also, in a manner of speaking, in play surgery and playwright physiotherapy; that is, someone who could help both play and playwright to breathe, walk, run, skip and jump again. It is a term, function and job that has existed increasingly regularly over the past century in European theatres and was explained, variously, as a director's sidekick, writer's confidant, defender of the status quo, radical intellectual, editor or an institution's artistic programming functionary.

Having worked as a dramaturg for the past 20 years I am now very, very sceptical of medicalising the term (such as 'play midwife' or, worse, gender stereotyping it as the 'angel of the playhouse'), but am not at all sceptical of the word or of the scope of the task. It is, though, a word with a history. We have already discussed the history, development and problematising of a few inherited words, but not yet 'dramaturgy'. 'Text', for instance, comes from Latin and emerged from the practice of weaving strands together to make a whole thing. 'Playwright', a compound noun from the early sixteenth century, saw a thing—the play—joined with the working-class trade

THOUGHT FIVE I DRAMATURGY

of making that thing, à la shipwright or wheelwright. When Ben Jonson coined it, it was not, however, intended as a compliment (he considered himself, as a poet and observer of classical rules, far above such a lowly craft). Similarly, dramaturg is a compound noun derived from ancient Greek. There is, surprisingly, no direct link to Aristotle or his *Poetics*. And unlike the word 'playwright', 'dramaturg' was invented in a spirit of great optimism.

A playwright was invited into a new Hamburg theatre company in 1767 to be its resident dramatist and the term was first deployed in that context. The plans were grand, indeed the company's founders sought to change German theatre utterly. In this wider context the coining of a new word for a new job was but loose change, a synecdoche for the innovations yet to come. The new Hamburg enterprise with Johann Friedrich Löwen at the helm hoped to raise German theatre 'to a dignity' which it had so far failed to achieve. Without his intervention he worried that 'we will never see German drama emerge from its infancy'. Löwen's new company was to be supported by a consortium of Hamburg patricians, independent of Church and government, with the ambition to school an acting ensemble, enlighten the citizenry and award playwriting prizes for staggering, landmark new works of German theatre. Ultimately, it would elevate German theatre as a whole, especially with prestigious critic and forward-thinking playwright Gotthold Ephraim Lessing handpicked for the role of resident dramatist, or 'official theatre poet'.

A playwright, editor and translator already known in literary circles as a tough critic of the status quo, Lessing (1729–1781) had started two, and edited three, separate theatre and literary journals, published books, pamphlets and broadsides and demolished reputations (notably of then leading critic J.C. Gottsched). He, like Löwen, bemoaned the bifurcation of 'German' theatre (including opera) into low comedy and high dramatic art saturated in French and Italian conventions. Lessing declined Löwen's offer—Lessing did not consider himself a 'poet', not feeling 'within myself the living spring that works itself out' and 'breaks forth out of its own strength into such rich, fresh, clear streams'[1]—but he nevertheless joined the venture. His revised role was '*die Critik*'. Lessing planned to write essays on the works presented, lecture the actors and the good burghers of Hamburg on theatre history, translate or adapt plays where necessary and be the in-house, as well as the public, critic of the actors, the choice of repertoire and the quality of the writing. Together, Löwen and Lessing's hope was to construct in Hamburg a true national repertoire and a model German theatre that civilised, as it was itself civilised.

Lessing explained that 'the better portion of the public' had given their approval 'both within and without the city' for the company's exertions for 'the general good'. In addition, it was not going to be run by an absolutist actor–manager but rather that its benefits would emerge organically, like cultivating a garden, because 'an association of friends of the stage have laid their hands to the task'. Beyond that, together, these 'friends' had 'combined to work according to a common plan for the public good'.[2]

The political context of this is important. At the local level, Hamburg was, unusually, a 'free city' ruled by a senate of private citizens and not beholden to a monarch and their taste or whims (Prussia's Frederick the Great revered Voltaire and decried the German language as 'coarse and almost barbaric' and had stingingly rejected the well-credentialed Lessing's application to be his official librarian). This makes Lessing's employment of those two powerful phrases—'a common plan' and 'the public good'—especially piquant. In Lessing's view theatre must not be ad hoc or show-by-show, or made simply to entertain and divert people's attention, but rather proceed with a plan, a core part of which was social reform, for theatre must play its part in a crucial moral and aesthetic renewal. For Lessing theatre must set ennobling, edifying and discerning standards: the 'mediocre should not pretend to be more than it is'. On the one hand, theatre could set high standards for art, providing an example for all to reach for, and 'to judge from'. On the other hand, and this goes to the wider political context, theatre could also become a democratising influence, a 'good' for all of the people, not just the elite. Lessing goes even further, valorising the authenticity of their audience's views, declaring that the audience's 'voice shall never be contemptuously ignored, its judgement shall always be respectfully heard'. Radical rhetoric indeed with Europe still 20 years from revolution and 50 from the first beginnings of universal male suffrage. He acknowledged that 'the steps are many' and that 'everything consequently cannot be done at once' but that

> The audience's voice shall never be contemptuously ignored, its judgement shall always be respectfully heard

the goal was nothing less than 'the climax of perfection'. As for 'matters of expense', nothing was to be 'economised' and indeed Löwen guaranteed that all of their workers' salaries and pensions would be covered by the theatre, guaranteeing more time on art and less on the quotidian concerns of everyday living.

Lessing himself was a true optimist about the company's new mission. While reference to 'optimism' may have pained him (his essays are full of bile directed at playwright and polymath Voltaire, author of the picaresque novel *Candide, or Optimism*, published just eight years prior), both Löwen and Lessing commenced the assignment full of grand ideals; indeed, like Candide, they hoped for the best of all possible worlds. Lessing may have disliked Voltaire's dramatic work but from our standpoint they were both self-declared members of the same optimistic vanguard, a loose school of philosophers and artists (Locke, Leibniz, Montesquieu, Rousseau, Hume, Franklin, Diderot, Kant, Moses Mendelssohn, and so on) who saw themselves as part of a movement to modernise society and civilisation, its art, lore, laws, politics and religious adherence. For them 'progress' was as much a literary process as an historical inevitability. This goal was a radical aim, a truly Enlightenment project.[3]

Lessing's first essay was given away free on the day the Hamburg theatre opened—in it he claimed that he would provide a 'critical index' of all plays performed, accompanying 'every step made' by the 'art of the poet or the actor'—but after that, it was a schilling an essay. Of course he also needed to give his 'journal' a title. He explained that he had one model, and two possible titles, in mind.

THOUGHT FIVE / DRAMATURGY

For the title he considered borrowing a word used by Aristotle, the ancient Greek word for 'teachings' or 'education' (that the Christian Church had co-opted), 'Didaskalia';[4] but he also contemplated the use of the merger of the ancient Greek word 'drama' with another ancient Greek word deriving from work, function, task or worker, 'ergon'—from which we in English now have ergonomic, organise, energy, surgery, the name George, even synergy. Lessing chose the compound word, a word that had emerged from Ancient Greek and then been adopted recently into Italian, French then German.[5]

As for the model of an ideas-based practical theatre journal—other than his own extensive reading and experience as a journalist, editor and critic—Lessing had been impressed by a German colleague's writings on a National Theatre (in Denmark), Johann Elias Schlegel, and commended readers to him in his essays. Schlegel saw the Danish National Theatre as a forum for the nation's finest intellects. He likened it, and 'the people', to two stones relentlessly grinding against one another, with one inevitably sharpening the other. Schlegel praised the ancient Greeks but deplored how 'Germans had made the mistake of indiscriminately translating all manner of comedies from the French ... so they have turned their theatre into nothing other than a French theatre in the German language'.[6] This call to Germanic nationalism—Germany was itself still 100 years from a political reality—accorded deeply with Lessing's own views.

Armed then with a title, *Hamburgische Dramaturgie*, and a Danish ideal of a National German Theatre, Lessing embarked upon his 'dramaturgy' in May 1767. So sanguine was he about the venture that Lessing auctioned off his own library to underwrite the publishing house that would print his essays on an ongoing basis. His contribution to the Hamburg enterprise would be an idiosyncratic critical register, didactic supplement, aesthetic and cultural survey, quite-interesting-fact smorgasbord and nationalist screed all rolled into one. Lessing's essays, collected together over his time there and known in English as the *Hamburg Dramaturgy*, are a more or less real-time analysis of the venture as it unfolded.

Lessing spent the better part of two years writing the essays (sometimes weekly, often more, increasingly less, 104 in total) on their actors, the plays performed and the challenges raised that he thought important to discuss, diagnose, dissect and demystify. His ability to quote freely from Ancient Greek and Roman sources, from French, English, Spanish and other contemporary plays and writers, make his impressions and observations feel candid, wise and waspish. He is philosophical but also particular, as happy to discuss Plato's *Republic* as a scene from *Electra* or even the various weaknesses of the Hamburg Theatre's own productions. The essays display him at his best—perceptive, passionate, honest and witty— but they are also both quixotic and mercurial.

When it became evident (very quickly) to Lessing that the actors were not objective packets of phenomena, but people with feelings whose performances got worse the more they were criticised, his critiques of their performances ceased. He stopped reviewing performances altogether after essay number 25, focusing instead on certain repertoire plays in a running critical commentary that was scholarly, polemical, but also fragmentary and often unfinished.

This is the difficulty! I here remind my readers that these sheets are to contain anything rather than a dramatic system. I am therefore not bound to resolve all the difficulties I raise. My thoughts may seem less and less connected, may even seem to contradict themselves, what matter if only they are thoughts amid which may be found matter for individual thinking! I only want here to scatter *Fermenta cognitionis*.[7]

As with his earlier reviewing work, Lessing was strong on opinion. He devoted almost fifteen essays just to Voltaire's *Mérope* and its errors, inconsistencies and lacunae; included a multi-essay takedown of Thomas Corneille's *Le Comte d'Essex*; continued his opposition to French neo-classicism; and praised the English and Spanish traditions, most especially Shakespeare.[8] Above all else, he praised Aristotle's continued relevance to his contemporary theatre in some detail.

One of his chief tasks, a responsibility he makes reference to throughout the *Dramaturgy*, was to rescue Aristotle from the formal strictures, solemnity, artificiality and ornamentation of French neo-classical drama, and from the Three Unities. Just as the French Academy had used Aristotle—and the ancient drama more generally—to authenticate their narrow dramatic choices, so Lessing used him to celebrate action, story and non-heroic realism:

No nation has more misapprehended the rules of ancient drama than the French. They have adopted as the essential some incidental remarks made by Aristotle about the most fitting external division of drama, and have so enfeebled the essential by all manner of limitations and interpretations, that nothing else could necessarily arise therefrom.[9]

He also pressed the case that Voltaire and his imitators belonged to a now dated, former age of the theatre.

These digressions into dramatic theory expanded over the course of the essays as his vision of a dynamic, responsive, practical critical register of the Hamburg enterprise itself receded. Lessing's detailed analysis of a model German theatre company from the front row, as it were, was increasingly derailed, partly because of his own predilection for digression:

> In truth I pity my readers who promised to themselves in this journal a theatrical newspaper as varied and manifold, as amusing and comical as a theatrical newspaper should be. Instead of containing the story of the plays performed, told in short, lively and touching romances, instead of detailed biographies of absurd, eccentric, foolish beings, such as those must be who concern themselves with writing comedies, instead of amusing, even slightly scandalous anecdotes of actors and especially actresses, instead of all these pretty things which they expected, they get long, serious, dry criticisms of old well-known plays; ponderous examinations of what tragedy should or should not be, at times even expositions of Aristotle. And they are to read this? As I say, I pity them; they have been grievously deceived.[10]

It was, however, more problematic, irrespective of his circumlocutory prowess, that there were real challenges within the company itself: Lessing needed increasingly to pad his 'journal' because the theatre company members were not enamoured of his 'critical' efforts; the company went on tour to Hanover for four months, leaving him

THOUGHT FIVE I DRAMATURGY   83

with little to discuss, which may also explain why some of the plays
he discussed were never even performed at the Hamburg Theatre;
what it did perform were almost entirely French plays in translation,
making discussion close to impossible on new German national
drama, except as an ideal; company infighting was intense; Löwen's
plans for regular performances of new plays flew in the face of the
mostly French repertoire that the acting company were experts in
and loved for; plus, one leading actress described Lessing as having
spent more time at the buffet than in the stalls. Ultimately, audiences
dwindled. It was soon evident that the Hamburg enterprise failed to
match its own rhetoric and it closed within two years.

Löwen blamed Church opposition and financial problems;
Lessing blamed the audience. It is truer to say, however, that it simply
failed as a commercial venture and of the twelve businessmen who
had invested—a couple of them did so just to support one of the
leading actresses, Sophie Hensel—their leader Abel Seyler could
not bail them out as he has already been close to bankruptcy at the
Hamburg enterprise's very commencement. Indeed, Lessing's final
batch of essays was published as the company itself went under.
Overall, Lessing was circumspect. He acknowledged that while
the collection of essays was not 'wholly that which I promised to
make them', he concluded that, on balance, they were 'something
different and yet I think nothing worse'.[11]

Lessing never worked as a company dramaturg again but over
the subsequent 20 years books on dramaturgy appeared, mimicking
Lessing's title, in Vienna, Mannheim, Leipzig and another in
Hamburg, along with works by Johann Schink and Adolph
von Knigge.[12] Lessing had changed the landscape for discussion and

analysis of theatre, its form, purpose and modality. Powerful further signs of change saw playwright, poet and physician Friedrich Schiller appointed dramaturg for the Mannheim Theater in 1783; poet, romantic and critic Ludwig Tieck (1773–1853) as Dresden Theatre's dramaturg in 1824; and Ellen Franz the dramaturg for the hugely influential theatre of Saxe-Meiningen in 1873 (when she married the Duke). Lessing was praised as a 'genius' by Goethe and was highly regarded by Ibsen and Bernard Shaw, with Stanislavsky crediting him as among the greatest influences in Western drama. Lessing's work was also inspirational for Erwin Piscator and Brecht who employed dramaturgs in their theatres, and of course for Heiner Müller, himself an institutional dramaturg before becoming artistic director of the Berliner Ensemble. The word and its function had quickly developed imitators, early adopters and soon occupied its own niche meaning and function: a worker in the drama, supporting, polemicising, arguing, analysing, explaining, attacking, educating, vivisecting, pleading, provoking.

Having worked regularly as a dramaturg, I have often been 'invited' to hear people's thoughts on what dramaturgy might mean, entail, and, most particularly, derail. As it has been articulated to me, a dramaturg is: unnecessary; a meddler; historically invisible; a writer and researcher, often of essays, but for context only; a stooge, flunky or bouncer for the management; a luxury; someone there just to take out the trash; an institutional traffic light (mostly amber, tending red); Stalin's blue editing pencil; a nutty professor; mere marginalia; Pandarus, Pangloss and Polonius rolled into one pompous mess; a keeper of the stone tablets; a bureaucrat; a dark

THOUGHT FIVE | DRAMATURGY

magus, practising only behind closed doors; or a word technician. A job, then, but mysterious, unclear, of confusing practical application, with unreliable training and opaque methodology. Stories abound of plays ruined by the intervention of a dramaturg. Considered an expert, their expertise is uncertain, arcane and potentially calamitous; aesthetic police, but who watches the watchers?

Without wishing to locate an originating moment for the dramaturg's initial obscuring in English-speaking theatre, in John Willett's otherwise fine translation of Brecht's *Dialogue aus dem Messingkauf* in 1965 (though the actual selection and editing of the text has been critiqued by scholars as problematic), he defines a dramaturg as a 'literary odd-job man'.[13] At about the same time Kenneth Tynan, newly employed at Laurence Olivier's novel National Theatre of Great Britain, sought to have dramaturg as his job title. It was denied. Perhaps these instances were in that British director's head when I asked about dramaturgy?

In Brecht's text, however, the 'character' of Dramaturg is held in high esteem. In the character description of this colossal work— part-play, part-theoretical treatise, Brecht worked on *Messingkauf* for almost 20 years—the Dramaturg is described as 'at the Philosopher's disposal, and promises to apply his knowledge and abilities to the reconstruction of the theatre into the theatre of the Philosopher. He hopes the theatre will get a new lease of life.' Brecht elaborated on the role over the course of this document and in it the Dramaturg opens the play itself, welcoming the audience to the 'House of Fabricated Dreams'; reads and analyses play scripts; is a theatre scholar; and is a brilliant critic who runs discussions not in their office but on stage, the site of collaboration, construction and deconstruction, and performance itself. The Dramaturg's job is theoretical, historical, practical, experimental and intellectual and is someone Brecht considered an active agent of change, a self-reflexive truth-teller who uncomplicatedly shares theatre's illusions.

Such optimism and such a wide remit can be set against the mere 'odd-job man' and the more general anxiety, anger or antipathy as to the definition, existence and orientation of the concept, or the history and practice of dramaturgy itself. Indeed over the past 20 years there has been a tremendous growth in publications on the practice and the concept.[14] Across a number of journals, conferences, workshops, curricula and books, the scope and scale of dramaturgy and its purview has continued to grow, becoming at once more intricate as it is more and better understood. Excitingly too, the task has expanded beyond the always uncertain job description of main-stage theatre literary manager to include the practices of curation and devising, begun to be deployed in other disciplines such as dance, new media, works in translation and architecture, and to embrace analysis of systems of management and of institutions themselves.

Simply put, the specific, professional role of dramaturg can include tasks such as producer, festival director, programmer, curator of experiences across and through an institution, writer of program and marketing material, researcher, stage manager, in-house critic, literary manager, leader of Q&As, workshop scribe, somatic witness, cultural advisor, dialogue partner, outside eye, new play and playwright development specialist, 'mentor, friend, compass, memory, fellow traveller, mediator, psychologist'.[15] Theatre scholar Theresa Lang sees the role as a present tense verb—as doing something—rather than as just a noun, that is, as something described, circumscribed and settled.[16]

Dramaturgy, beyond being considered merely the dramaturg's to-do list, concerns the theoretical and practical composition of the work, or event, as a whole: its architecture, tone, fabric, weave, politics, ontology, loops and tangles, and the manoeuvring of bodies, language and objects across both time and space. A work, a thing, a process, a gesture or a place can have a dramaturgy, not at all dependent on a dramaturg analysing it into existence, though the dramaturg's expertise elucidates the efficacy, intricacy and competing and complementary fields of that dramaturgy, or dramaturgies. Marianne van Kerkhoven referred to dramaturgy in 1994 as the 'twilight zone between art and science', alluding to its concern with a production's internal structure; Elinor Fuchs has described its interest in the organic structure of the performance; and Mark Lord as 'the intellectual *mise-en-scène*'.

One recurring focus for both the dramaturg's task and dramaturgy—partly to offset the suspicion that dramaturgy has now grown to consider itself the analyst of everything performative, or that it is entirely esoteric critical theory—is that of sharpening it, or limiting it, to the real world practice of posing questions. Suzanne Bell, the New Writing Associate of the Royal Exchange Manchester, in her paper on winning the Kenneth Tynan Award in 2019, encouraged dramaturgs to 'keep asking difficult questions'.[17] In the paper she quotes both Swedish-English dramaturg Hanna Slätne—'the more we can question, the more robust the process'—and Kenneth Tynan: 'curiosity about people is merely the beginning, that curiosity must be sustained even when the end has been reached'. Mark Bly, an artist many consider 'the father' or even 'godfather' of American dramaturgy (he defers instead to Anne Cattaneo as its 'mother'), recently spoke to the core value of a dramaturg's 'questioning sprit' to underline its value and function.[18] Michael Mark Chemers observed in his 2010 book on dramaturgy that, as people ask 'what the #$%@ is' a dramaturg, so must dramaturgs keep asking themselves the same question.[19]

For some, however, simply asking questions is just too open-ended an exercise to generate any real critical or practical valency. A volley, or otherwise, of questions opens dramaturgy, and the work itself, up to useless, diffuse, exhaustive or reductive inquiry without politics, context or transparency, or a sense of its multiple dynamic textural inputs. We may kid ourselves that just asking questions is phronetic, that is, prudently seeking practical wisdom,

As people ask 'what the #$/@ is' a dramaturg, so dramaturgs must keep asking themselves the same question

and that, while we may feel good asking smart questions about a play or performance event, it may do little for our collaborators, colleagues, spectators or the work itself, or those forgotten or excluded from the table, workshop or rehearsal room. Worst of all, a fusillade of questions can silence, confuse, patronise or belittle the writer. Beyond that, when does or should one's dramaturgical

THOUGHT FIVE | DRAMATURGY

intervention, questions notwithstanding, take place? Creating a performance is a temporal, physical exertion, but are we dramaturgs when a show is being constructed, well in advance but without the input of other makers, or when deconstructing its kinaesthetics only after the show has been completed? Any questions we might ask are entirely dependent on our positionality in our temporal and physical reality.

In my neck of the theatre woods, new plays are intensely sensitive to, and dependent on, their initial conditions. As someone with an opinion, some training, institutional power and a broad vocabulary, I as a dramaturg can easily destabilise a new work, even with tiniest of perturbations, just because of the dynamics of the various systems in play, for any such agitations are magnified, amplified and distorted within them. Rather than asking questions, which can sometimes have this effect, I tend to approach any new work asking myself four questions first. I call it the 'KGML Test', something that marks my first dramaturgical intervention and involves me checking my own head before opening my mouth, putting pencil to paper or frowning at a first read. The 'K' relates to Sarah Kane and reminds me to muse upon whether I am smart enough or courageous enough to fully comprehend the work I intend to analyse. The 'G' refers to Gutenberg, Johannes, the inventor of the printing press. We have a cognitive bias, a heuristic, that favours printed plays. Looking at a PDF of an imperfectly formatted play in a font I do not like (both ridiculous, I know, but both the source of unconscious bias) can often make me dislike a play or, at the very least, see it as a series of problems, blind to my own impaired judgement. The 'G' also reminds me that by far the majority of plays I have ever read are published, themselves the result of many collaborators, oftentimes including a number of audiences, and themselves a product of significant investment, very unlike an unfinished new play. The 'M' is for Montaigne and his *cri de coeur*, 'What do I know?' There is no better *aide-mémoire* for excoriating one's ego than the sixteenth-century French ex-judge and inventor of the word 'essay'; it is also a prompt to work harder, think better, analyse deeper, understand more intuitively. And the 'L' is a must for any dramaturg, the obverse of asking questions, that is, to listen. Should I have anything to say, I try and boil my responses down to just three thoughts, observations or provocations (unless requested to do otherwise, and I am always happy to provide a quick 5,000 words!).

Perhaps my most sustained active dramaturgical conversation has been with theatre and dance dramaturg Ruth Little. She was my mentor when I was her reader at Griffin Theatre over 20 years ago and we have kept in touch on the limits of dramaturgy as commonly practised. As I went down one path, so Ruth became interested in living systems. She contends that live performance itself is a living, evolving system, an assemblage united by the regular interactions and interdependence of the objects passing through it. For her, dramaturgy is a study of process and pattern, metaphor and analogy, an exploration of the changing behaviour of systems. In any of our performance explorations, rehearsal rooms or discussions, we each observe complex and unpredictable patterns across different levels of scale. What tools or theories do we have in theatre to understand this depth, multiplicity and complexity? Literary theory, at least to

THOUGHT FIVE | DRAMATURGY

1980, is not up to the mark. Nor are Aristotle, Castelvetro, Freytag or Stanislavsky.

Ruth observes that we need a new way of knowing and recording that takes into account: a) that all living systems exist somewhere between chaos and stasis, life and death, order and disorder; b) that we are all remembering animals, compulsively constructing narratives based on our pasts; and c) that we are also sense-saturated embodied selves living only in the present. At these rough edges, these thresholds, places of entanglement, friction and biodiversity, are moments of suspension, emergence and transformation. Such moments are when we begin to feel or react. They exist at the margins of consciousness or performance, that is, in the space between performer and spectator, individual and institution, stage and auditorium, humans and the natural world, the arts and everyday living. Far from being marginal, however, such interactions, dramaturgical in essence, exist at the core of our practice and our everyday ways of being. Such thresholds, junctions, aporia or vanishing points, are places of encounter and exchange, learning and unlearning. Ruth points to the threshold of land and sea as an example, that is, the intertidal zone. It is replete with resourceful, flexible, convivial organisms, a place of opportunity and resilience. Referring both to the work of Austrian philosopher Ivan Illich and American scholar Donna J. Haraway, she extrapolates that our dramaturgical aim must be to enter into actual, meaningful encounters, to speak and speak back, gesture, give and receive;[20] or what philosopher and political theorist Jane Bennett calls engage in 'wiser interventions'.[21] For

Ruth, dramaturgy works with perception and meaning and is itself a relational practice, a way of understanding and navigating the creative process at the edge of chaos, with awareness and care. We are working not towards a destination but involve ourselves in a process of navigation, improvisation and maintenance. In these marginal, always already negotiated spaces we need to privilege the multi-vocal, the provisional, the flexible, the participatory, the humble, the curious and the generous.

Working recently with Australian First Nations poet and novelist Ellen van Neerven, and despite all my awareness and care, I nevertheless realised that I was at the boundary of current dramaturgical thinking. Their searing, heartfelt and devastating portrayal of the breakdown of a mother–daughter relationship because of the psychic and visceral impact of casual, structural and institutional racism, magnified by the Australian legal system, exposed the fact that dramaturgy needs to be refigured from a post-colonial First Nations perspective. Similarly, working with emerging writer Grace Feng Fang Juan, a native Mandarin speaker, on her play written entirely in Mandarin, it was self-evident that there is much more work to do in the processes surrounding intercultural dramaturgical futures. With comic writer Alistair Baldwin and his as yet unfinished comedy on 'orphan diseases' (diseases that afflict only a very small number of people so rarely attract pharmaceutical company investment in their cure), again it was apparent that a new dramaturgy was required to fully comprehend the experience, perception and impacts of people living with a disability.

From the very start 'dramaturgy' was contingent, borrowed from

THOUGHT FIVE | DRAMATURGY

three other languages, filled with hope and idealism, scholarship and bravado, but also bursting with in-built contradictions, interdisciplinary glee, mess, frustration, disappointment and opportunity. Both the words 'playwright' and 'dramaturgy', far from emerging from the minds of a so-called genius, exist instead at the unstable meeting point of creation and execution, theory and practice, noun and verb, ideal and insult, language and linguistics, gesture and breath, frustration and possibility. The artists who invented, and continue to reinvent dramaturgy, actively wrestle with all that came before, not seeking to dominate and over-determine, but, in order to make space for the new, to disturb what currently exists and to better comprehend all the variable fields at play in a vocation that was, until recently, neither a legitimate profession nor a respected industry (Schiller was appointed dramaturg at the Mannheim while on the run from the Duke of Württemberg). Dramaturgy describes work that is dynamic and subject to change, itself dynamic, brawling with emotion, history, viscera, error, accident, constraint and the empty space, always itself on the margins, adjacent to dissolution and invisibility.

Being at the edge reminds me of Edgar Allan Poe and a column he began in 1844 for the periodical *Democratic Review*, 'Marginalia'.[22] Early on he admitted that, when purchasing books 'I have always been solicitous of an ample margin' because of 'the facility it affords me of penciling in suggested thoughts, agreements, and differences of opinion, or brief critical comments in general'. There, in the margins of someone else's work, he felt free to respond to it, unfettered; 'we therefore talk freshly—boldly—originally—with abandonment—without conceit'. Poe was aware that he existed on the edges of both plagiarism and vandalism, but he did so for 'theatrical and self-aggrandizing purposes'. Existing in an ample margin but also in conversation with each work's core, marginalia is an artistic activity that is critical, immediate, internal, negligible, bold and without conceit, a provisional home for thoughts, agreements, differences of opinion. It sounds like a splendid, if necessarily temporary, provisional model for dramaturgs and dramaturgy.

THOUGHT SIX
Brain soup: Story and the mind

Recently, storytelling has seen a renewed interest as a targeted sales tool and management strategy. Part of the reason for its recent re-adoption by the corporate world is new brain science.[1] Of course the linking of story and sales is hardly new—Benjamin Franklin's *Poor Richard's Almanack* was an early example, but think also of *The Michelin Guide*, *The Guinness Book of World Records* and more recently Red Bull Media. But recent TED Talks and YouTube clips of persuasive speakers, often salespeople, doctors, or both, with exercises, books and training seminars to hawk, have each drawn on the latest scientific discoveries about narrative, that telling stories stimulates specific mental cues. Not only that, these mental cues can apparently be quantified and controlled. As told in books such as Charles Duhigg's bestseller *The Power of Habit*, the triggering of such cues is at the centre of our warning and reward systems, and once we get to know the new science in its finer detail, so we can control our brains better.[2]

These recent discoveries make reference, in particular, to the fact that storytelling stimulates the production of certain chemical neurotransmitters (scientists have now identified more than 500 unique ones). Their emergence, variously, gives us an edge. As neurotransmitters promote the exhibition of distinct behaviours, so stories that target certain ones drive us into action, action that will ultimately make us better, happier, smarter, more productive, and buy more. As a result, storytelling itself has gone under the microscope. The following stories, however, while not often discussed in rehearsal rooms, should be of intimate interest to theatre makers.

In the 1920s it was confirmed that messages passing through the brain are chemical, not electrical, but quite how these chemicals all work, work together and interact continues to be a subject for ongoing scientific exploration. The relevant 'storytelling' neurotransmitters—at least as they are being spruiked at present—are dopamine, oxytocin and endorphins. By telling stories of suspense, for instance, our brains are stimulated into dopamine production, leading to better focus, motivation and memory retention. In weaving together stories of sadness, oxytocin is synthesised, fostering greater generosity, empathy, trust and bonding—apparently, it is especially evident in new mothers.[3] With endorphins, it is by and large the sharing of humorous stories that stimulates their production, great for relaxation, feelings of euphoria, creativity and the reduction of pain.

Storytelling can also encourage the manufacturing of certain hormones, most especially cortisol. Like adrenaline, which is made immediately when an ancient part of our brains, the amygdala (not the 'reptilian brain' as it is sometimes called, but it does date from a shared ancestor) perceives a threat, so cortisol is manufactured by the hypothalamus, the pituitary and adrenal glands in response to real or retold distress. Immediately, adrenaline increases the heart rate and elevates the blood pressure. Then cortisol, in just a few minutes, increases sugars in the bloodstream, enhances the brain's use of glucose and increases the availability of substances that repair tissue as well as supplying the large muscles with ready energy. In the short term, cortisol is great at putting us on high alert, and good for focus, memory and attention.

For marketers then, stories can act like giant funnels. First, by being scary or shocking—adrenaline, cortisol—they capture an audience's, or a customer's, attention. Next there is suspense—dopamine—for attention, focus and immediate awareness. Finally, with a bittersweet, heart-warming end—oxytocin—or a funny punchline—endorphins—feelings of relaxation, reward and creativity drive changes in action, and sales.[4]

Scientist, entrepreneur, TED talker and self-described neuroeconomist Paul J. Zak is especially bullish about using story to motivate action and change behaviour. In a 2009 study he asked his subjects to watch two video clips.[5] One told the story of a father whose son is dying of cancer, the father especially enjoying the limited time he has to play with the dying son. The other concerned a father and son walking through a zoo going from cage to cage. According to the study's findings, those who reported preferring the first clip (most subjects) also felt empathy for those characters, and were found to have 47 per cent more oxytocin in their bodies that those who did not feel empathy. In the study, researchers then gave money to the subjects to spend as they pleased, with the option of donating to cancer research. Later, analysing the subject's brain chemistry, heart rate, skin conductance and respiration (and what they did with the money), Zak's team found that the subjects who produced the highest levels of cortisol and oxytocin were more likely to donate money generously. Those with intranasal oxytocin increased the generosity of offers by 80 per cent over the placebo. One way of reading this information is that triggering brain chemistry through targeted stories can motivate people to action, accurately predicting the percentage of those who will not only do a thing, but spend their money.[6]

That there is a relationship between story, behaviour and action may not be such a surprise for writers, dramatists in particular. Some writers, besides questioning the above research's veracity or methodology, may be perplexed at reducing life's rare and sublime 'a-ha' moments—a story's wonder, empathy and mystery—to dependence on fMRI scans and brain chemistry. Emeritus UCLA Professor of Psychology Shelley Taylor has even cautioned: 'It's never a good idea to map a psychological profile onto a hormone; they don't have psychological profiles.' Plus, in the long term, excessive cortisol production has now been proven to lead to anxiety, immune troubles, digestive problems, heart disease and weight gain; and oxytocin, far from being the 'hug hormone' or the 'cuddle chemical'—and this is less well-noted in the popular science articles—can also lead to increased feelings of envy, tribalism, distrust and ultimately diminished cooperation.[7] The sales power of the 'cuddle chemical' is a great story though.

Less interested in sales, neuroscientist, fellow TED talker and scholar Suzana Herculano-Houzel asked a more basic question: are our brains special? Intrigued by our enduring belief that they are, and that we are too, she both metaphorically and literally dissected the human brain.[8] Not satisfied with the assertion that our brains were somehow biologically noteworthy—even though humans consider themselves rulers of the world, being able to travel anywhere on, or beyond, it—Herculano-Houzel looked to quantify the brain. In her 2016 book she challenges a number of common misconceptions and now superseded 'truths', most particularly about the human brain's evolution and common measures as to its distinctiveness (relative size or weight; relationship between brain and body mass). She suspected that 'specialness' might result from high neuron count (the information processing units of the brain), especially so in our cerebral or prefrontal cortex. To prove it, however, she needed to accurately count the number of neurons in our brains. Previous approximations were guesstimates and unable to account for the brain's lumpy, heterogeneous, asymmetrical reality. The only estimate that existed—and Herculano-Houzel could find no legitimate source for it—was that the human brain had 100 billion neurons.[9] To find the answer, Herculano-Houzel turned to, of all things, household detergent.

Brain cell membranes, but not cell nuclei, dissolve in detergent. That process, which is of course much more complicated than just soaking a brain in Palmolive, allowed Herculano-Houzel to count neurons from different creatures' brains, then eventually, from different parts of the human brain. Herculano-Houzel said that as she was developing the technique she was haunted by images of brains in standard kitchen blenders hitting ceilings. She called it making brain soup—and it does seem to have a passing resemblance to chicken and vegetable soup—though they later named it the 'isotropic fractionator'. On the one hand, she demonstrated that we are not special—our brains have evolved much like other mammals, with a total neuron count of an appropriate (for our size) 86 billion (elephants have 257 billion!)—but, on the other hand, we humans do have a remarkably densely packed prefrontal cortex (the African elephant has a mammoth total number of neurons, but 98 per cent are in its cerebellum, not its cortex). We possess 16 billion neurons in our cortex, whales and cetaceans have on average 9 billion, chimpanzees 6 billion, elephants 5.6 billion, giraffes 1.7 billion and capybaras (a large South American rodent) 0.3 billion. While this is pioneering work, Herculano-Houzel never questions the equating of cognitive capacity with 'intelligence', nor the quantity of neurons as a raw explanatory number as against neural organisation (particularly the way brains have become modular and run in parallel networks), nor properly reviews bird 'intelligence'.[10] Nevertheless, 16 billion is an impressive number, allowing for a lot of empathy, attention, focus and story, or, as the neuroscientists call it, executive function. One of the most fascinating aspects of her book relates to the energy 'cost' of our brains and how crucial cooking our food was (that is, pre-digesting it) to the evolution of large, densely packed brains, unlike our larger gorilla cousins whose brains are surprisingly small for a primate.

Detergent notwithstanding, understanding and mapping the brain's functionality, as it relates to mental and behavioural activity, has only really been possible during the twentieth century because of developments in neuroimaging (PET scans, fMRI, EEG, ECoG, MEG, NIRS).[11] Historically humans have sought a measure of understanding—despite Aristotle's belief that intelligence lay in the heart—through trepanning, inferences drawn from the critically injured, such as Phineas Gage who famously survived a rod through his brain, and other investigative operations.[12] It is with the new forms of imaging, however, that we can now view the mental 'arithmetic' occurring—where words are formed, where lies are generated, where religious sentiments fire—but such a 'view', though quite interesting, comes with serious caveats. 'Hot spots' are revealed (changes of levels of oxygen in the blood for instance, or blood flow—actually first observed in Italy, 1868 and studied further in London in 1890—or glucose utilisation) but co-locating exact thoughts with exact areas or moments remains a challenge, and does not take into account other harder to detect brain changes (fluxes of ions across lipoprotein neural membranes for instance) that occur in tandem with those bigger 'thoughts' and that may be just as necessary.

In the 1930s, Montreal neurosurgeon Wilder G. Penfield (writing later with Theodore Rasmussen) electrically stimulated the brains of epileptic patients (163 at first) while operating on them, observing a direct correspondence between the part of the brain they were stimulating and a part of their body (the patients were conscious). To make it clearer, they later drew diagrams, both in two and three dimensions, publishing the findings in 1950.[13] When represented as a small 3D human, or 'homunculus' as Penfield called it, the hands, lips and tongue are immense, especially compared to the tiny feet, hips or chest. Why? A disproportionately huge amount of our brains (motor and sensory cortexes) are devoted to communication and the making of social connections. Penfield's work can be misapplied (on grounds of overreach, but also brain cells generally do more than one thing) but this is a profound insight for humans, especially artistically inclined ones: as we have evolved, our brains are mostly busy with gesture, touch and speaking and interpretation of those things. For Penfield, studying the mind was important, 'more vast than outer space', but even despite his work the 'secrets of the mind are hidden still'.[14]

Not wanting to drive us down a crude, biologically over determined superhighway, or into an expensive, exclusive, marketing seminar, there are rich discoveries in recent thinking on the brain and the mind that we ignore at our peril.[15] For instance, new research on brain activity reveals some staggering numbers: how do we make sense of the possibilities of our 86 billion neurons and their 100 trillion possible interconnections enabled by the 1,000 proteins at each connection point? We are, roughly speaking, capable of carrying out one petaFLOPS of logical operations every second (a thousand trillion, or a 1 followed by 15 zeros!).[16] But we must be careful to not make the brain sound like a computer, which it self-evidently is not. Computers process information; their memory

THOUGHT SIX / BRAIN SOUP   103

is physical, literally stored somewhere, able to be retrieved; they
run by rules set in programs steered by algorithms; the patterns
they recognise are through the movement of bits of information
coded into small chunks that get switched around actual silicon
pathways. We have chemicals, senses and reflexes. Playwright and
scholar George Zarkadakis has observed that humans have always
compared our brains to the latest, contemporaneous example of new
technology, whether that was hydraulics, a telegraph network or
complicated machine, so regularly making the comparison between
brains and computers is perhaps kind of inevitable, if ill-advised.[17]
Nevertheless, while the brain is a masterpiece of complexity, it does
have its limitations. Indeed, technologists remain optimistic about
hacking our limited 'hardware', potentially changing the nature of
being human.

    Is any of this, though, the story of your brain?[18] Numbers and
neurotransmitters? Logic-machine meets fleshy filing cabinet? Does
a shred of that capture nuance or story, Darwin's observation of
'worms crawling through the damp Earth' or Warsan Shire's 'if it will
keep my heart soft, break my heart everyday'?[19] If this momentary
turn to numbers, chemistry and FLOPS feels too 'left-brain', then it is
worth dwelling briefly on the work of Iain McGilchrist. Psychiatrist,
philosopher and literature scholar, he wrote his 2009 intellectual
bestseller *The Master and His Emissary* in order to analyse how our
brain's fundamental hemispheric division has played out, in his
view, across human history. Far from a simplistic paean to the right
brain (home of feeling, vision, experience, spirit) over and against
our current culture's seeming left-brain chauvinism (the focus on
analysing, reasoning, percentages, abstraction, efficiency), the story

he crafts is of the interconnections, stability and deep productive complexity of our brains, yet it is a system increasingly marked by imbalance.

Our two brain hemispheres, connected by the 200 million neural fibres in the *corpus callosum* (Latin for 'tough body' and the largest connective pathway in the brain), are physically unequal. Our right cerebral hemisphere is larger than the left, with more neurons (though the left brain hemisphere overall is larger in most people), the right is also slightly twisted in front of the left (the Yakovlevian torque) and each hemisphere responds differently to neurotransmitters, their surface gyri are different, even their cell structures are dissimilar. As the brain evolved in our predecessor animals, McGilchrist explains, it sought to complete two interrelated but separate tasks: we need to eat, and not be eaten. That this is apparent is most evident in birds. A bird's left hemisphere, or right eye, focuses on getting the seed in the grit, while the left eye (and other senses) is attuned to the surroundings, the bigger picture, and potential predation. This mechanism set the template for all bi-hemispheric animals, with each hemisphere attending to separate but interconnected activities. Intriguingly, the right hemisphere is the 'master' in McGilchrist's central metaphor, instructing the left brain to grasp, to categorise, to divide and conquer. The right brain is also silent, for in humans it does not have control of speech (or significant gesture). As an example, the left brain, when attending to faces, only examines the lower half of the face, never the eyes. Yet the right brain does read the eyes, and brings the information gained by the left (language, lips, volume and so on) together with broader contextual information, to form an opinion, a response, an emotion. He characterises the different but interlaced aspects of our hemispheres thus: 'The right hemisphere, the one that believes, but does not know, has to depend on the other, the left hemisphere, that knows but doesn't believe.'[20]

McGilchrist's work is intricately detailed, finely observed and revelatory. Wary of over-simplification with respect to each hemisphere's function—commenting, for example, that both visual imagery and language are served by both hemispheres, as is the imagination—McGilchrist is fascinated by the manner with which things are done, our ways of attending, the processes we discern of 'responsive evocation' or 'transformative echoes'. At its most simple, the left brain manipulates well, seeing the world as mechanical, while the right sees context and the broader perspective. For example, the right understands that pursuing happiness makes no sense, as it cannot be pursued successfully, and can only emerge as a by-product of such a pursuit. That, however, does not stop the dogged, head-on left brain from hunting down happiness, primarily through material possessions and seeing the world as a resource to be manipulated (which it is very effective at) for our (ultimately short-term) gain. In McGilchrist's view, the right brain's 'emissary', the left brain, thinks it knows better than the right, its 'master', and continues to try and re-make the world in its image, to the detriment of the wider context, the ungraspable and the irrationally imaginative. An imbalance between the left and the right may also explain certain mental illnesses.

I first came to consider the work of the brain, its mysteries and our mind's inner workings through reading *The Mystery of the Cleaning Lady* by Sydney novelist Sue Woolfe.[21] Woolfe was writing her third novel (*The Secret Cure*, about a young man with a severe stutter), but also struggling with it, and began to read other writers on their writing. She and novelist Kate Grenville had already interviewed Australian writers about their writing process in 2001, producing *Making Stories*, a classic of Australian literature. Much of the overseas literature on writing, however, was penned by men and most of it was a variation on the theme of 'a writer writes'. This did not describe Woolfe's practice or experience. Maybe she was just a vessel for her characters' voices? Maybe the book 'wrote itself'? Did she steal it? Wolfe increasingly saw her mind as unruly, easily distracted, ill-disciplined and mired in indecision in comparison to more hard-nosed, harder-working scribes. She was surprised when they described the regimen of their writing process, the business-like hours they kept, how their process was orderly and uncomplicated and how they rejected as romantic claptrap the idea of an irregularly descending muse. Perhaps her mind was doing 'something wrong', something that jeopardised the creative work itself? That began a journey into what would, for Woolfe, become life-changing and affirming, because the more she read and researched, the more she discovered that her idiosyncratic process was the real story of creativity, and we were built that way.

Becoming bogged down, ideas arriving unpredictably, often in flurries, being inattentive and escaping 'work' to a gallery or just getting out for a walk in a park, was more common than she had expected. It also turned out that the mind did not stop 'working' when she stood up from her desk. A random call for an interview from a Wollongong PhD student alerted her to the burgeoning wealth of research into the brain, story and creativity. While the field has exploded in recent years, perhaps led by Hungarian-American literature scholar Mihaly Csikszentmihalyi and his books *Flow* and *Creativity*, for then PhD student Christopher David Stevens it began with studies on 'insight' from the 1930s and 1940s by E.D. Hutchinson and then the mid-century work of US cognitive psychologist George Kelly.[22] In Stevens' developing thesis, and his bibliography, Woolfe was especially compelled by the notion that creativity and insight took place when the brain toggled between two modes of thinking: abstract and specific, reverie and rationality, analogy and distinction, difference and sameness—what Kelly termed 'loose' and 'tight construing'. Neurons and activated transmission patterns are not thinking, but this movement, for Woolfe, underlay the mind's generation of emotion, feeling, thinking, action and the generation of story. It also held the key to the way she knew she wrote. More recent work by Oliver Sacks and by Antonio and Hanna Damasio confirms what many also suspect: that the brain and the mind do nothing without the cooperation and participation of the body; hence, walks, galleries, staring out the window while making a cup of tea, but also the feeling that the story is coming from the fingers or the belly, that it is not being dictated only by the brain. Logic and structure have a place in story, but only later, only after the artist has floated through what the Damasios refer to as our 'somatic markers'—thoughts and emotional states with distinctive physical traits but few conscious referents. This sounds not dissimilar to postulates of the philosophy of mind of Susanne Langer and her non-semantic forms of thinking, our 'bristling sensual record of the instance'.[23]

From here, with this lateral shift from forebrain function to ways of attending to insights drawn at the emergence of cognitive psychology, it is not a huge jump to the pioneering work of psychologists Amos Tversky and Daniel Kahneman. If their names are not familiar to you, their work may be through the big Hollywood films *Moneyball* or Kahneman's bestselling book *Thinking, Fast and Slow*. Though Kahneman and Tversky wrote about psychology, it was in economics that their work was awarded the Nobel Prize in 2002. Two men, almost entirely opposite in temperament (optimist/ pessimist, loud/quiet, tidy office/chaotic office, witty/considered and tending gloomy, bold/cautious), they came together when Kahneman complained to the swaggering Tversky that he did not believe a word of Tversky's guest lecture. Chalk and cheese, they then collaborated, forever changing the nature of our thinking about judgement and decision-making. How? Between 1971 and 1979 they published just a few papers, each demonstrating with startling clarity, how regularly and confidently we make mistakes. They alerted us to a common tendency, that when asked difficult questions most humans use simplifying operations, 'heuristics', that yield adequate answers but often rely on inaccurate information and result in errors in judgement and found that the resulting errors can be anticipated, specified and categorised. Their questioning of the descriptive adequacy of our classical behavioural models (especially economics, but also psychology) provided a cognitive template

THOUGHT SIX | BRAIN SOUP

that explained our flawed judgement, without recourse to 'innate' irrationality. Kahneman and Tversky's eight papers went on to change psychology, economics, medicine, the law and public policy debates, and spawn a new discipline, behavioural economics.[24]

New and interesting cognitive biases now run to the hundreds, from anchoring to zero risk, the Zeigarnik effect to authority bias, loss aversion to

> What Kahneman and Tversky made clear is how poor are we at making sound and effective judgements

hyperbolic discounting—with some of the most well-known being availability bias (we use readily available information instead of fact), conclusion bias (we marshal only the facts that support a conclusion we have already drawn) or confirmation bias (we are influenced by irrelevant information; for example, that an attractive political candidate will be good at their job), but my particular recurring fear is endogeneity bias (confusing correlation with causation, missing the wood for the trees, with a feedback loop! We can fall prey to this in rehearsal when we lose a sense of the external and start making excuses for what is not working). What Kahneman and Tversky made clear is how poor we are at making sound and effective judgements, a humbling fact and in some ways, bad news for us humans (and that with our tendency to 'bad news bias' notwithstanding). And while we are not 'systematically flawed bumblers', sometimes doing better than rivals, such all-too-human behaviour could not be described as 'optimal'. Indeed Tversky once said: 'People are not so complicated. Relationships between people are complicated.'[25] They revealed an everyday world in which people did not act in their best interests, and, worse, that egregious errors, often of inferential folly, were systematically made by judges and juries, doctors and patients, statisticians, engineers, economists, by us all. Kahneman recently reflected, with the imminent publication of a new book on 'the Noise problem', on what might perhaps be our greatest flaw of all: overconfidence.[26]

One final thing to note is that our human minds are tangled in an as yet unresolved tussle, something that was perhaps touched on glancingly in the discussion of Sue Woolfe's book, and that concerns artists and their wellbeing. In the face of underemployment, professional uncertainty, artistic 'failure', anxiety and depression, where do artists find a measure of resilience? Our Western culture holds that on the one hand the artist is a cliché, starving, tortured by visions of 'tongues of fire' over fjords like Edvard Munch, beset by 'attacks of melancholy and of atrocious remorse' like Van Gogh, or just frail victims of life itself, as Virginia Woolf or Sylvia Plath are sometimes mischaracterised—that is, that we expect our artists to suffer for their inspiration and their principles, that this is the cost of great insight.[27] On the other hand, there is also a growing intolerance for artists' sensitivity, seen as 'snowflakes' who refuse to comprehend that art is only worth what someone will pay for it, yet they want government handouts as they wait for the muses to descend, and, worse, that in demanding arts funding by government they are inherently making a form of special pleading, in essence that artists are anti-democratic in their quest for 'welfare for cultural elitists'.[28] Do artists sacrifice their wellbeing for their art? Are artists

THOUGHT SIX | BRAIN SOUP   111

bad at life? Is it something imbalanced in their brains? Recent studies, thankfully, have put data where anecdote used to reside, especially on the neural correlates of creative thinking and any correspondence with mental illness.[29] I am heartened also by the proliferating number of studies on the value of art, and art-making, to the brain. Indeed I even found a webinar on the beneficial effects of art on the brain, that is, 'neuroaesthetics'. The webinar features Susan Magsamen, founder of the International Arts and Minds Lab at the Johns Hopkins University School of Medicine, and Kelley Remole, a neuroscientist from Columbia University's Zuckerman Mind Brain Behaviour Institute. Rather than trying to sell me something, they were evangelical and proselytising about neuroaesthetics for health and wellbeing. The webinar is free.[30]

While none of the above explains why we humans prefer fiction to non-fiction,[31] nor show us where the story neurons are, it does hint towards the extraordinary ingenuity and near immeasurable possibility with which we are gifted, enabled by the surprising degree of our brain's plasticity and our mind's mutability. While revelatory of our overconfidence, bias and errors, it seems to me that recent neural studies—themselves sometimes subject to bombast and hyperbole—also offer a liberating narrative. Indeed new studies have even revealed that exposure to fiction delivers us from binary thinking—that is, from seeing the world as black and white, us and them, right and wrong. Fiction encourages us to review particulars, metaphor, representations and literary non-referential narrative beyond considering just a very limited number of functions and viewpoints; lived experience of multiple perspectives, as occurs in theatre or novels, breaks us away from what some researchers have called 'cognitive closure'.[32] Computer simulations may 'help us get to grips with complex problems such as flying a plane or forecasting the weather' but our experiencing of 'novels, stories and dramas can help us understand the complexities of social life'.[33]

Seventeenth-century doctor and polymath Thomas Browne described humans as a 'Noble Animal', 'splendid in ashes, and pompous in the grave', as brave as we are infamous.[34] He observed that our brains were a paradox, 'for in the brain, which we tearme the seate of reason, there is not anything of moment more than I can discover in the cranium of a beast'.[35] He, just like Kahneman or McGilchrist well after him, questioned our ability to embrace complexity and our immediate future—'A Dialogue between two infants in the womb concerning the state of this world, might handsomely illustrate our ignorance of the next'[36]—yet he himself revelled in our ability to make portraits of the 'invisible fabrick'.[37] We are 'wonderfull in what we conceive' but we are far more so 'in what we comprehend not'. Always deferential to God's supreme knowledge, he quietly rejoiced in our all-too-human folly 'to pry into the maze of his Counsels' where there is 'no thread or line to guide us in that labyrinth'.[38]

This perhaps foolhardy neuro-optimism reminds me of some dialogue in Merlynn Tong's as yet unperformed play *Golden Blood* (programmed for 2020 at Sydney's Griffin Theatre, and an MTC Next Stage commission, it was another COVID casualty and will hopefully resurface in 2022). A recently orphaned older brother, Boy, and younger sister, Girl, bicker, he dismissive of her youth, cupidity and

THOUGHT SIX | BRAIN SOUP

inexperience. Boy is in awe though of Girl's imagination: 'You have the creative brain'. Late in the play, when Girl has lost her way, Boy takes her to his inner sanctum, the source of his wealth and power, in order to inspire, but also to encourage her to solve both of their increasingly intractable problems: 'You have been like a big lazy bear in hibernation/ But I think it's just your brain that has been sleeping you know/ It's time to wake up.' Boy wants to 'wake up' her brain because ultimately it will mean 'We can be free'. His at times solipsistic logic and appalling business plans across the play rather resemble a pyramid scheme, but it is also the kind of sanguine 'neuro' economics that I can subscribe to, to wake up our brains, and keep doing so, in order to be free.

Thought Seven

Elementary particles: 'even with a thought / The rack dislimns'

Recently I had the good fortune to travel to the Northern Territory and walk, for my first time, around the base of Uluru. I have seen it in images, still and moving, most of my life and yet I was shocked at coming into contact with it up close. Far from being smooth and regular, a familiar red monolith, it defied description at almost every other metre, itself utterly strange, vertiginous, disorienting, perpetually playing tricks with my eyes. Its patterns of erosion, sedimentation, markings, fissures, moving shadows, nooks and crannies, gorges, protected waterholes, sacred men's and women's sites, caves, surprise shelters, pot-holes, etched and carved stories, and its changing colours, defied my powers of comprehension, a solid rock infinitely and infinitesimally complex. Sacred to the Anangu people, it, along with everything in the landscape, is the source of Tjukurpa (law and culture):

> We have no books, our history was not written by people with pen and paper. It is in the land, the footprints of our Creation Ancestors are on the rocks. The hills and creek beds they created as they dwelled in this land surround us. We learned

from our grandmothers and grandfathers as they showed us these sacred sites, told us the stories, sang and danced with us the Tjukurpa. We remember it all; in our minds, our bodies and feet as we dance the stories. We continually recreate the Tjukurpa.[1]

Extending deep into the ground like an iceberg, Uluru is roughly 500 million years old, is about ten kilometres around the walking track at the base, and reaches up almost 350 metres, higher than the Eiffel Tower, Melbourne's Eureka Tower or New York's Chrysler Building. Coming face to face with this level of complexity, particularly knowing only a tiny number of the rock's stories, with multiple histories written on, into and across it, I encountered Uluru as alive with intricate detail beyond my ken. A symbol of Australia, a synecdoche for Australian history (that is, ancient but only recently 'discovered' by white people—in 1873, briefly, and then again in 1893), this sandstone, feldspar-rich rock is also now synonymous with the 2017 Statement from the Heart, a powerful invocation to empower Australian First Nations people, an incitement to walk from 'base camp ... in a movement of the Australian people for a better future'. Complex, indeed.

Staring straight at complexity is sometimes a dumbfounding experience—are we equipped to comprehend so many variables, patterns and interwoven and interweaving elements? As I mentioned in *Thought Five*, we are often frustrated in theatre by our limited descriptive tools, our provisional, often two-dimensional explanatory models or reliance on fuzzy concepts and anecdotally received 'theories'. Such a frustration, or just plain limitation, has

THOUGHT SEVEN / ELEMTARY PARTICLES

fired much recent formally ambitious dramatic writing and its dramaturgy, but we have yet to settle on a mode, methodology or set of theories that captures performance and new plays with the complexity or ingenuity with which they are conceived and written. In this final *Thought* I will examine four models for scrutinising change, each welcoming dynamism and volatility. In their disparate ways, each offers tantalising possibilities for holding space for the inarticulate and disordered, comprehending simultaneity and operating multiple processes coherently.

If theatre, famously, is powerful yet ephemeral, grounded but evanescent, a moving architecture of breath and air, is there an instructive analogy or model for it? Scratching my head on this about fifteen years ago I looked up and—Eureka! Clouds! Of all the things around us, they are utterly everyday, yet they have defied philosophers, priests and the wise for thousands of years—until very recently—as to an adequate understanding of their shapes, patterns and secrets. The weather itself is confusing enough, contradictory, hieroglyphic and cruel,[2] but clouds are delightful, whimsical, portentous, confounding, and may now be a key part of a geoengineered climate-changed future (marine cloud brightening or cloud seeding!). How can they be understood, or managed, if they are perpetually in motion? Is there a theory—Aristophanes notwithstanding—of clouds?

Throughout history looking up at the sky has provided humans with a rich and manifold source of signs, clues and analogies: a source of omens, prophecies, gods, forewarning, harmony, the zodiac, technical thinking, and now a second-nature description of big data, the network of servers on which most of us rely. Ever mutable, clouds and their mysteries, along with thunder and rain, have long been recorded: on papyrus and clay, ancient bamboo measures and charcoal gauges; in the Taoist pantheon as part of the Ministry of Thunder; in the Torah's books of the prophets as evidence of God's vengeance; and in Norse mythology with clear classifications of different gods, their specific clouds and mist. Thales of Miletus, Anaximander and Democritus each propounded proto-scientific, not divine, explanations as to clouds' origin and motor (a water cycle of moving vapours, an ocean of air under pressure, snow and sun each playing a part). So too Aristotle, when he wrote his *Meteorologica*, an explanation of the atmosphere and its dynamism, which he argued was a result of the four elements' interaction and interchange, a process of paired exhalation and inhalation. The treatise's first description, beyond the preamble, is of the life cycle of clouds.

In another of Aristotle's works, *On Dreams*, clouds also appear, but in a rather more poetic, slippery and troublesome likeness. He equates dreaming with 'seeing' centaurs in the clouds—that is, something grasped only momentarily, perhaps an hallucination, or worse (for Aristotle), misplaced sensory perception. For some early modern Europeans clouds were a joke of nature, *lusus naturae*, but for medieval occultist Heinrich Cornelius Agrippa they reflected, as in a distorting mirror, events on Earth.[3] Shakespeare too turned to clouds in a number of their guises: they can literally hide the sun; they symbolise loss, death, betrayal and instability; they are revelatory of our imaginations and our characters; but they are also emblematic of uncertainty and transformation. Hamlet befuddles Polonius with them—'A weasel? A whale?'—but for Roman triumvir and Cleopatra tragic, Antony, they are a seventeenth-century Rorschach blot, however anachronistic:

Sometime we see a cloud that's dragonish,

A vapour sometime like a bear or lion,

A towered citadel, a pendent rock,

A forked mountain, or blue promontory

With trees upon't that nod unto the world

And mock our eyes with air. Thou hast seen these signs?

They are black vesper's pageants ...

That which is now a horse, even with a thought

The rack dislimns and makes it indistinct

As water is in water. (*Antony and Cleopatra*, IV, xiv, 2–11)[4]

Was the ability to see identifiable patterns in clouds purely in the imaginative eye of the beholder, or was it prescience? Did it mean something or nothing? Here Antony refers to clouds as neither due to chance nor God's command, but recognises in them his own gruesome rending and erasure.[5]

René Descartes, writing only 30 years later, entirely rejected as mere superstition such an approach to the heavens. He instead sought to find, as he noted in his *On Meteors*, the 'real cause of everything wonderful above the earth' in the 'hope that if I explain their nature here ... one will no longer have occasion to admire anything about what is seen or descends from above'.[6] In his way, Descartes sought to quantify discussion of air, fog and clouds, snow and rain, storms and rainbows—even beating Isaac Newton to the division of white light through glass into colours—by pure denotation.[7] That is, a cloud means nothing more than it is: particles mechanically following rules. He believed in relying on one's intuition, but a scientific rather than imaginative one:

> By 'intuition' I do not mean the fluctuating testimony of the senses or the deceptive judgment of the imagination as it botches things together, but the conception of a clear and attentive mind, which is so easy and distinct that there can be no room for doubt about what we are understanding.[8]

Rejecting *probable* cognition, Descartes resolved to acknowledge only what is known and incapable of being doubted. Despite his certainty and conviction, however, clouds and their perpetual dance, even if only mechanistic, remained as yet ungraspable by science.

Debate continued for another couple of hundred years— with Ferdinand II of Tuscany, Robert Hooke, Prince-Elector of Mannheim Karl Theodor, and Lamarck all devising now mostly forgotten taxonomies of clouds—until a little known 30-year-old manufacturing chemist, Quaker and amateur cloud-gazer, Luke Howard, gave a speech, 'On the modifications of clouds', to the Askesian Society in December 1802.[9] In less than an hour Howard described his system to name and classify clouds. It remains in use today. Worried that his topic may be perceived 'a useless pursuit of shadows', he explained that far from an ever varying 'sport of winds', clouds could in fact be defined. He proposed some basic types, not hundreds or thousands, but just three, with a fourth acting as a modifier. Taken from Latin (as with most natural history terms) there were *cirrus* (Latin for fibre or lock of hair), *cumulus* (pile, heap or aggregate) and *stratus* (sheet, cover, spread, layer) clouds, with *nimbus* (the Latin for raincloud) a rainy variant of all three. The especial insight here was that Howard assembled the many moving pieces so that, in his proposed explanatory system, they contained all of their permutations and combinations—*cumulonimbus, stratocumulus* and so on. They retained their individuated multiple forms, but could also be aggregated to a very limited number of basic types, alive to the transience of the atmosphere.

Up until the late seventeenth century, mathematics was in general unable to manage, measure or quantify such transience. Maths could calculate smooth objects and objects that were still, but given that almost everything around us is in motion, this was a serious drawback with respect to its applied relevance or usefulness. Curiously, the method to determine rates of change, motion and dynamic change, or as physicist Richard Feynman described it, 'the language God talks', was conceived of by two people at almost exactly the same time. What is it? For most of us it is a barely remembered series of equations to do with parabolas from high school maths: calculus. More than a language or a series of equations, however, it is a powerful system of reasoning, the construction of long, dense chains of logical inference. While it may seem remote and almost entirely abstract, James Clerk Maxwell used calculus in the late nineteenth century to take the electrical discoveries of Michael Faraday and André-Marie Ampère and produced the wave equation (which, mathematically, explained how a changing electrical field generated a changing magnetic field, and vice versa), calculated the speed of this wave—the speed of light—and proved incontrovertibly that light was an electromagnetic wave! Cue the twentieth century! How, exactly, complex, symbol-filled equations can represent real fields of force and real dimensions as well as describe changing real-world phenomena remains tough to explain—Albert Einstein got it of course, writing in 1936 that the 'eternal mystery of the world is its comprehensibility'—but calculus allowed humans to predict the unknown, track curves, motion and change, and, for a mathematician or physicist, it makes the complicated simple (they may even say, elegant). It is used now to analyse electricity, heat, light, harmonics, acoustics, astronomy and geography; is used in photography, artificial intelligence, robotics, video games, fluid flow, ship design, geometric curves and bridge engineering; and to predict rates of radioactive decay in chemistry, birth and death rates, gravity and planetary motion.

It starts, of course, with a paradox—Zeno's. Nine of his paradoxes have been preserved (mostly via Aristotle), all intended to prove, perhaps slightly perversely, that motion, change and plurality are absurd illusions relying on seeming impossibilities such as infinity. The two relevant paradoxes here are Achilles and the Tortoise, and The Arrow. In the first, Achilles races a tortoise and, giving it a head-start, he can never catch it despite his virility, because of the increasing, ultimately infinite, gradations of distance he needs to cover in order to overtake it. In the other, every moment of the arrow's journey sees it at a particular point in time, occupying that moment on that journey; but being at a particular point assumes that it must be at rest as it passes through that point in time, hence, rather than moving forward, it is perpetually suspended and can never reach its destination. Zeno breaks up both distance and time to micro-units to mock the inconsistencies apparent in allowing for pluralities. Regardless, infinity provided a clue for subsequent thinkers in Europe, China, the Middle East and India to discover, ultimately, methods that calculated how curves changed and how to determine the area under a curve. By slicing it into infinite pieces, or by counting an infinite number of N-sided polygons abutting the edges of circles, spheres, parabolas or ellipses, the motion or shape can be calculated.

Ingenuity is key here, possibly a little obsession, and certainly 'too much delight' in pursuing complex ideas—that this is so is evident in the case of Newton's first attempt at discovering the area under a parabola, a result he chased down, by hand, to a mere 'two and fifty figures'.[10] Both Newton (natural philosopher) and Gottfried Leibniz (linguist, theologian, legal scholar, courtier, mathematician and philosopher) accused each other of plagiarism in a slanderous public dispute as to who was its inventor that lasted almost 20 years, six years beyond Leibniz's death.[11] Looking to determine the mechanisms of change, each asserted that their method be given priority as correct and invariable. They cast each other as flawed, as thieving and as gluttonous for fame, despite between them creating pristine methods that tracked motion and change over time (good for understanding planets and cannonballs, or later, blood flow, electrical signals, space craft and epidemics). Neither believed in infinitely small (or large) things, but used them as thought experiments to allow for the discovery of new and better ways of understanding motion and change over time, what Newton called 'fluxions' and that for Leibniz began with: $\pi/4 = 1 - 1/3 + 1/5 - 1/7 + 1/9 \dots$

Is there not something here for theatre, not simply the quest for better prediction or analysis, but for better methods of fathoming dynamic change over time? Far from the idea being too arch, physicist Paul Dirac fell in love with one particular piece of calculus before he could prove its utility or accuracy. Ultimately building this under-explored aspect of transformation theory into an entirely new way to view both maths and the universe, the idea led to countless theoretical and practical advances (in 1927, Dirac used calculus to unite general relativity and quantum mechanics, and accidentally proved anti-matter existed!). To this day mathematicians praise his hunch, and his calculus, as 'achingly beautiful', concise and with powerful physical consequences, conceived by an intuitive genius.[12]

Sounds like a great show.

Is there not something here for theatre, not simply the quest for better prediction or analysis, but for better methods of fathoming change over time?

If clouds are too fleeting and calculus too tough, esoteric and maybe too internecine or enclosed for us, a phenomenon we immediately gravitate towards, know very well or jokingly think of when we recall time in a theatre, is chaos. Far from it being, however, descriptive of a haphazard free-for-all of disorder and confusion, recent studies of chaotic systems are compelling. And, in a way, chaos, in science, is the opposite of calculus, to the extent that it generally starts with simple rules. Chaos (sometimes chaos theory) as a discipline developed because of the observation of formal

THOUGHT SEVEN / ELEMTARY PARTICLES   125

simplicity ultimately exhibiting random, surprising and extremely complicated behaviours. Do the new theories of chaos, that is, the analysis of dynamic systems, perhaps provide a useful model, guide or incitement for theatre?

If so, to gain a measure of its generation, we must go back to discussing the weather. Individual molecules of air and water conform to basic laws, yet the weather is anything but simple, as Edward Lorenz found out in the early 1960s when he modelled an early weather forecasting computer program. Initially with twelve variables (temperature, wind speed, pressure, convection and so on, and using calculus), and an early computer[13] he, with the help of both Margaret Hamilton (who later wrote the software for Apollo 11 and Skylab, not the actor who played the Wicked Witch of the West) and Ellen Fetter, ran and re-ran simulations on the program. (Lorenz wrote the equations that governed it himself, since he had trained as a mathematician before ending up in meteorology.) Lorenz apparently went to get coffee and the printer rounded up one of the variables from .506127 to .506 to save space on the page. That tiny emendation dramatically transformed the simulation itself. As Lorenz described it in 1963, one of the most important properties he observed of slight changes to a system's initial conditions was 'its instability with respect to modifications of small amplitude'.[14] With a plethora of accurate statistics and some complicated maths, they showed that the weather was not only following Newton's laws, but was also stochastic—a system that exhibited a random pattern, making accurate prediction very, very difficult (the word 'stochastic' itself derives from ancient Greek, a guess, conjecture, a target for archers to try and shoot at). That the weather was hard to predict is hardly a bolt from the blue, but he did not stop there.

Following the maths, they graphed how tiny changes (in an already simplified computer simulation) had huge, erratic consequences in certain systems. Lorenz, Hamilton and Fetter clearly demonstrated that if a system had the capacity to vary, it would rarely repeat or be predictable—with divergent iterations the result not just of bad human data, but the interdependence of the system itself. A similar problem had been observed during the early development of radar by Mary Cartwright in the early 1940s. This unpredictability, despite our wish for it to be otherwise, or because of classical expectations of a clockwork universe, was instead a common part of natural systems—algal blooms, Saturn's rings, salmon in a fishery. Irregularities in weather and oceanographic phenomena such as eddies and advection, indeed any aperiodic behaviour, were also observed obeying certain geometric shapes when subjected to squeezing, stretching, pressure, friction and air resistance. Perhaps the really surprising thing was that while they were unpredictable and all varied, all potentially chaotically, they did so within certain limits, indeed they looped strangely around these limits (the Lorenz attractor).

That Newton's promise of the predictability of an already determined universe was under challenge was an understatement, but what became known as the butterfly effect has attracted both hype and common misconceptions. This new scientific discovery began to reveal something nature had previously kept hidden, or that was perhaps obscured by the observers' desire for regularity, neatness and order. A Robert Redford character, in 1990's *Havana*, claimed that scientists could calculate the odds of a hurricane in the Caribbean as a result of a butterfly flapping its wings in China, and missed the whole point of the theory, that is, that some systems are just too complex to be certain of anything.[15] Patterns could be observed but their secrets remained recondite. Perhaps Jeff Goldblum's chaos theorist Dr Ian Malcolm in *Jurassic Park* gets closer to the nub of it, for Hollywood that is, when he muses that 'life escapes all barriers ... Painfully, perhaps even dangerously. But life finds a way.' When Lorenz, Hamilton and Fetter had plotted their results on a 3D graph, Lorenz later described it as 'an infinite complex of surfaces'.[16]

While Lorenz was sceptical of overconfident scientific certainty, having seen systems explode with disorderly and ultimately 'chaotic' behaviour, observers of 'chaos' during the 1960s and 1970s pursued the obverse aspect of its unpredictability. That is, that although certain systems do vary wildly, they do so only within limits and in discernible, recognisable patterns. That chaos follows patterns seems quaint, almost ironic, yet it does so—extraordinary, surprising and creative—with intricate, astonishing identical detail, in the same way, at every level of scale. When thinking about randomness it is likely that we will think of the bell curve, or even Benford's Law, and that while there may be random outcomes, they will spread according to predictable patterns. Such simplistic assumptions of predictability were challenged by, amongst others, a mathematician interested in dynamical systems and economics, Stephen Smale, astronomer and mathematician Michel Hénon, and mathematical physicists David Ruelle and Floris Takens, all of whom generated results that revealed deep evidence of a dynamic, turbulent and stochastic universe. Australian theoretical physicist Robert May taught applied mathematics but became interested in the biological sciences, specifically the dynamics of population change. It was a numbers problem that had vexed him since his postgrad days, a problem similar to the one that Lorenz and others were beginning to compute, the problem of non-linear dynamics and how for some systems, far from settling and reaching equilibrium, curious things started to happen as parameters changed only slightly. For May it was the bizarre way a graph charting a relatively straightforward equation began to bifurcate, bifurcate again, and suddenly exponentially diverge as the parameters grew from just below the whole number one, to the number three. An electrical engineer turned physicist, Mitchell Feigenbaum, observed similar behaviour in period doubling, ultimately creating a constant that described it, just prior to the onset of chaos.

Benoit Mandelbrot, a young IBM odd-job man and outlier working in the late 1960s and beyond, had also noticed a stochastic universe, populated with chaotic patterns. A displaced Paris-educated Polish-born Lithuanian and self-described 'black sheep' who had taught economics, engineering and physiology, Mandelbrot had a real skill for seeing maths and geometry in three dimensions. In representing, graphically, what he observed in aggregating data of irregular phenomena—word frequency in linguistics, stock-market fluctuations, error bursts in message transmission, changes to the depth of the Nile, income distribution, cotton price variations—

THOUGHT SEVEN / ELEMTARY PARTICLES   129

he kept seeing a common geometric structure that was bumpy, jagged and irregular. Mandelbrot perceived that what was taking place at surfaces and thresholds, tracking a number of variables across the boundaries of competing dominions, was bizarre and once considered monstrous by earlier mathematicians. He was also fascinated by the way naturally occurring shapes were rough and seemingly random, something classical maths and geometry had smoothed out to idealised shapes. Coastlines and lightning bolts for instance are jagged, bumpy, rough, surprising

Breaking, scission and subdivision better described what he was seeing in his data, but also what he saw in the world

and seemingly infinitely detailed, akin to one of Zeno's infinity paradoxes. Flicking through his son's Latin dictionary, Mandelbrot came across the root of the word fraction, the words *fractus* and *frangere*, to break. To Mandelbrot, breaking, scission and subdivision better described what he was seeing in his data, but also what he saw in the world.

Running his diverse datasets through the powerful IBM computers where he worked—indeed he illustrated his book with then state-of-the-art late 1970s computer illustrations—what he revealed was most definitely a break with what people thought of nature, let alone what maths could describe or computers could trace. He observed geometrical processes—the Mandelbrot set relies on just $Z \rightleftharpoons z2+c$—in an entirely new way, their breaking down into tinier and tinier parts, fractals, patterns that were infinitely complex yet bound by finite edges, with patterns inside patterns. These recursive patterns, in the case of the Mandelbrot set—the twiggy, capillary, hairy edges of an odd-looking beetle, or a plus-sized clown with a hat and baggy pants—shimmer and, once magnified, reveal ever more detail, in what seems baroque, then rococo, then decadent Pre-Raphaelite filigree. These chaotic, delicate, wild patterns are just created by an initial equation with each answer then fed back into the equation—work pioneered by French mathematicians Gaston Julia and Pierre Fatou—with the patterns displaying self-similarity, a new, stunning and beautiful kind of chaotic complexity. Think snowflakes, trees, mountains, blood vessels, rivers, clouds. Mandelbrot had asked in the late 1960s how long the coast of Britain was, speaking to his ability to see levels and levels of complexity. Of this ability, which he called new intuition—to see something ancient and ubiquitous yet, thus far, hidden—he wrote:

> The cases this mathematics allows us to tackle, and the extensions these cases require, lay the foundation of a new discipline. Scientists will (I am sure) be surprised and delighted to find that not a few shapes they had to call grainy, hydralike, in-between, pimply, pocky, ramified, seaweedy, strange, tangled, tortuous, wiggly, wispy, wrinkled, and the like, can henceforth be approached in rigorous and vigorous quantitative fashion. Mathematicians will (I hope) be surprised and delighted to find that sets thus far reputed exceptional (Carleson 1967) should in a sense be the rule, that constructions deemed pathological should evolve naturally from very concrete problems, and that

the study of Nature should help solve old problems and yield so many new ones.[17]

Intuition, iteration, recursion, breaking with the past, wild claims, new shapes, surface dynamics, beauty, delight and pathology—this chaos is indeed starting to sound more and more applicable to theatre.

One final thing: complexity. Clouds, calculus and chaos are not complex enough so far, you cry! So, what about Shannon entropy, Zipf's law, Boolean networks, Fuzzy Markov decision processes or WolframAlpha?[18] Somewhere in between thermodynamics, information and computation theory, genomics, statistics and biology, there emerged in the 1980s and 1990s a new related series of conjectures as to the gap between data generated by certain systems and the laws or explanations that elucidate the interactions generating the data. What are, for instance, the emergent phenomena that led to language? Or the complex adaptive interdependencies of a rainforest? What of the ecosystem of specialised bacteria that we carry within us each day? Or stock-market fluctuations? Ant colonies? The immune system? The turbulent flow of air around a plane's wings, especially near the jet engine or aileron? How to explain the patterns of animal imitation and mimicry and associated chains of borrowing and translation, specialisation and growth? The flocking of birds in flight? Each instance, argues John H. Holland (himself simultaneously at a number of boundaries, a professor of psychology, electrical engineering and computer science), reveals evidence of diversity, recirculation, niche and hierarchy, and coevolution. Unlike chaos, which reveals evidence of a certain, surprising gyration and unpredictability, complexity theory examines systems that exist in between order and chaos. At the heart of these structures, also referred to as complex adaptive systems, are an agent or agents that adapt and learn through interaction, that build networks (of nodes, loops or cycles and edges) often in multidimensional communities, experience shock, produce variety, adapt, recombine, innovate, depend on conditional actions and porous boundaries, and often reproduce. For scientists, in observing them, it is as though they are observing games whose volatility or cascading details are rules they do not yet know. These are systems that explore in a seemingly unfocused way, yet that can exploit those explorations and discoveries in a focused way: perhaps even the basis for the genetic algorithm?

That this field is contentious goes without saying—some consider it pop science with no real explanatory power to yield a substantive contribution to knowledge.[19] Back in 1962, however, the brilliant American polymath Herbert A. Simon (another boundary rider, an expert in political science, psychology, management studies and economics, winner of a Nobel Prize and a Turing Award) effectively established the discipline by writing on the 'architecture of complexity', making the point that while physical, biological or social systems could not be expected to share more than 'nontrivial properties', they in fact did.[20] He argued that every complex system observed a hierarchy (in the sense of systems with successive subsystems, rather than a descending series of worker processes with a descending series of bosses) of interdependent components that exhibited complex interdependence at every level of scale. In considering 'cybernetics', emergence (systems in which the whole is more than the sum of its parts), the actual behaviour of adaptive systems, the use of feedback, and the need for homeostasis (the regulation and balance of maintaining life, that is, an artefact existing between creation and entropy), Simon implored his colleagues to 'provide the substance to go with the name'. Subsequent thinkers have since observed more complex, collective behaviour and that these systems not only adapt, but that they signal, internally and externally. Collective behaviour, diversity, recirculation, coevolution, interdependent networks, signalling—these too all sound like a way of thinking about theatre and about plays.

At the risk of getting in well out of my depth—'idle fancy or sheer ignorance', as Simon put it in 1962—it is perhaps worth noting, given the above, that the rules we use to grasp, predict and navigate our world are changing. What is happening in biology, mathematics, physics, computation and information studies should not be missed. We have so much in common: as the astrophysicist Mario Livio suggested, we all remain in awe just as we are all puzzled by humans and by the wider world; that is, we strive, we fail but still we learn.[21] Is the future in our bones?[22] These scientific archipelagos offer new ways of thinking, theorising and comprehending strange, tangled, wispy or wrinkled shapes, accelerating and surprising movements, and extant things, both imagined and real.

A youngish Ludwig Wittgenstein wrote: 'physiological life is of course not "life". And neither is psychological life. Life is the world.'[23] To capture cascading data with rigour, generate possibility with precision, suggest new combinations of the already known with the seemingly impossible, is the urgent imperative of all of us. Having started with rules at the beginning of this book, it is fitting that we now close in the realm of possibility, chance, entropy and emergence with some new rules, or, if not rules exactly, then with new protocols, customs, provocations and expectations. And interestingly, much of this work was begun by scientists themselves on the edges of, and in between, a number of disciplines. On thresholds and fuzzy edges—like Robert May or Benoit Mandelbrot, Mary Cartwright or Margaret Hamilton—sites of chaos, friction, dissonance, strange topologies; or as philosopher of science Nancy Cartwright calls it, 'the messy, mottled world we live in'.[24]

You may well ask whether, by making reference to chance, chaos and plurality, I am suggesting that theatre is pure disorder, a haphazard artform as without insight as the infinite monkey theorem.[25] Far from it. Making theatre takes talent, insight, persistence, reliance and great perceptive power, itself a perpetual process of movement, of breath, of learning and unlearning. Nor am I asserting that theatre, or the writing of a play, is just the result of, for instance, a Fuzzy Markov decision process. Markov processes, like plays, describe new and dynamic arrangements—often previously unknown, hence fuzzy—that evolve over time according to chains of probability, laws of movement and a sequence of prescribed decisions. Markov chains, however—more traditionally used to manage queueing systems or inventories than actors, stories or relationships—do not have memory. But playwrights, performers, even theatres, all do.

THOUGHT SEVEN / ELEMTARY PARTICLES

This should suggest to you great swathes of possibility and, certainly, models beyond those in two dimensions, already in libraries or clogging boulevard theatres. And this wondrous, strange, monumental task of bringing memory, action, free play, exchange, digging and finding, heroes and anti-humanists, chaos, heuristics, rigour, storms, vulnerability, complexity, randomness, loose and tight construing, history, our petaFLOPS and our stories etched on rocks or written by our feet, together, in a vital, interdependent, dynamic, unpredictable, foliated, turbulent and cascading process brings me great hope—that's how to write a play!

ENDNOTES

1   Fabiola Gianotti, quoted in *The Guardian* by Ian Sample, 24 Feb 2019 (https://www.theguardian.com/science/2019/feb/23/fabiola-gianotti-interview-director-general-cern-particle-physicist-large-hadron-collider); Ellen van Neerven, 'Sacred ground beating heart', in *Throat,* University of Queensland Press, St. Lucia, 2020, p 40; Caryl Churchill, *Escaped Alone*, Nick Hern Books, London, 2016, sc. 8; Emile Zola, 'Naturalism on the Stage', *The Experimental Novel*, 1881; William Shakespeare, *Hamlet: Prince of Denmark*, Act 1, Scene 5, ll:171–175; Augustine of Hippo, *City of God*, Book 11, Chapter 26; Ovid, *Metamorphoses*, Book 15; Pythagoras, 'Seasons of the Year', lines 234–236.

Introduction

1   The standard Go board has a 19×19 grid of lines, containing 361 points. At the beginning of the game Black starts with 181 stones, and White 180. The number of legal board positions in Go have been calculated to be approximately 2.1×10,170. To determine this result required raising a 'sparse matrix' of 363 billion rows to the 361st power. It took a supercomputer from March until December 2015 to determine the result. The resulting number is more than the estimated number of atoms in the universe! For more see John Tromp and Gunnar Farnebäck, 'Combinatorics of Go', 31 January 2016, available online: https://tromp.github.io/go/gostate.pdf.

Thought One

1   Gotthold Ephraim Lessing, *The Hamburg Dramaturgy*, Essays 101–104, 1767–1769, p.263. He also said, 'I acknowledge it exactly as Aristotle abstracted it from the countless masterpieces of the Greek stage.' Lessing commented that he had his own thoughts on 'the philosopher's poetics', but 'could not bring them forward here without prolixity'. See also Michael Anderson, 'A Note on Lessing's Misinterpretation of Aristotle,' *Greece & Rome*, vol. 15, no. 1, 1968, pp.59–62.

2   Aristotle fares less well in feminist analyses given his arguments that: women's virtue is to obey (men's virtue is to command); although women can be good characters, they are more likely to be deficient in

some key regard (*Poetics*, Chapter 15); women have fewer teeth than men; and that women contribute nothing but matter to their offspring. See Cynthia A. Freeland (ed.), *Feminist Interpretations of Aristotle,* Pennsylvania State University Press, University Park, 1998.

3   Aristotle, *Poetics*, Malcolm Heath (ed. and transl.), Penguin Books, London, 1996. For more explication (including both Greek and English, and over 600 pages!) see Gerald F. Else, *Aristotle's Poetics: The Argument*, E.J. Brill, Leiden, 1957.

4   Classical scholars often take into account Aristotle's other works in more wide-ranging discussions on the *Poetics*. Some of these other concepts include the five virtues of thought: *technê* (craft), *epistêmê* (knowledge), *phronêsis* (practical judgement, prudence), *sophia* (wisdom) and *nous* (awareness); also *dianoia* (thinking), *aretê* (virtue, but also a disposition for taking action), *lexis* (disposition to do something), *orexis* (desire) and *prohairesis* or *proaeresis* (choice, the cause of action).

5   Socrates first makes this distinction clear in Book 3 of *The Republic*; and classics scholar Stephen Halliwell explains that *diegesis* comes from a Greek verb meaning 'to guide/lead through'. Halliwell qualifies the difference between *diegesis* and *mimesis* as narration and acting-out, however, as an oversimplification, explaining that in neither Plato nor Aristotle are they presented as simple binaries. Epic poetry, for instance, uses at least three different registers: various characters speak, the poet/author speaks in their own voice, and there is direct narration. To make matters more complicated, neither classical philosopher ever defined the term *mimesis*. For more see: Halliwell, 'Diegesis–Mimesis', in the 'Living Handbook of Narratology', revised 2013, originally published in Peter Hühn et al. (eds.), *Handbook of Narratology*, Walter de Gruyter, Berlin, 2009, but now maintained and updated by Hamburg University Press here: https://www.lhn.uni-hamburg.de/node/36.html

6   Aristotle refers to *eleos* and *phobos* which are most commonly translated as pity and fear. The German philosopher Hans-Georg Gadamer preferred 'misery' and 'shuddering', the German philologist Wolfgang Schadewaldt 'lament' and 'horror', with playwright and dramaturg Lessing heavily critiqued in the literature for introducing Christian dogma by translating *eleos* as 'pity', a concept foreign to archaic Greece. Claudio William Veloso recently argued that many words commonly associated with the *Poetics* were never included in the original document at all: see Claudio William Veloso, 'Aristotle's Poetics without katharsis, fear or pity', in *Oxford Studies in Ancient Philosophy 33*, Oxford University Press, Oxford, 2007, pp.255–284. See also Boris Grkinic, 'Appraisal Theory and the Emotions Eleos and Phobos: A Contribution of Current Emotion Theory to the Interpretation of Greek Tragedy', in Saetre, Lombardo and Zanetta (eds.), *Exploring Text and Emotions*, Aarhus University Press, Aarhus, 2014.

7   For a more detailed discussion of *ethos* and *dianoia* ('thought') see Mary Whitlock Blundell, 'Ēthos and Dianoia Reconsidered', in Amélie

ENDNOTES 139

Oksenberg Rorty (ed.), *Essays on Aristotle's Poetics,* Princeton University Press, Princeton, 1992, pp.155–176.

8   For more on the meaning and connotation of *agon* see Debra Hawhee, 'Agonism and Aretê', *Philosophy & Rhetoric*, Vol. 35, No. 3 (2002), pp.185–207. As for 'protagonist' it most especially should be differentiated from the word 'hero' that, for the Ancient Greeks, meant a character who, at story's end, becomes semi-divine. See Charles H. Reeves, 'The Aristotelian Concept of the Tragic Hero', *The American Journal of Philology*, Vol. 73, No. 2, 1952, pp.172–188.

9   As with every other word mentioned in the *Poetics*, *hamartia* is a hotbed of multiple meanings. In modern rehearsal or classrooms it slips quickly into discussions as the hero's 'fatal flaw'. Aristotle did discuss '*hubris*' but only as a subset of *hamartia* and as it related to excessive or wanton violence, pride, insolence or passion, a character who takes an action that arouses shame.

10   *Muthos* is the origin of our word 'myth' but they are not at all the same thing. Then, a *muthos* was a true story that unveiled the origin of the world (and of humans). We tend to use the word now to mean a fable, or a commonly held story that is in fact false. In ancient Greece, great stories were conveyed orally through poetry, but in the seventh century BCE two new discourses emerged offering other modalities of story, history and philosophy. Both Plato and Aristotle wrote considering the use, power, form and function of each in turn.

11   Aristotle does mention performance at the end of the sixth chapter, commenting that 'the effect of tragedy is not dependent on performance and actors' and that the way a play might look on stage was not the grand business of 'poets'.

12   Castelvetro, from Maxim 9, in Daniel Gerould, *Theatre/Theory/ Theatre: The major critical texts from Aristotle and Zeami to Soyinka and Havel*, Applause Theatre and Cinema Books, New York, 2000, p.136. He was known by his rivals as 'the owl with big ears', *gufo*, a term of derision; and he chose the image of the owl on a vase (preferring the name of a different owl) in response to this criticism, as well as the Greek inscription '*Kekpika*', or 'I have judged'. For more on his emblem of choice see: https://www.emblemstudies.org/eotm003/

13   Hans-Thies Lehmann, *Postdramatic Theatre*, Karen Jürs-Munby (transl.), Taylor and Francis, London, 2006.

14   Lehmann, *Postdramatic Theatre*, p.69.

Thought Two

1   Shakespeare's company, The Lord Chamberlain's Men, produced a play c.1599, *A Warning for Fair Women*, that contained a similar anecdote about a woman confessing to the murder of her husband, having seen it acted by some travelling players: 'Wherein a woman that had murtherd hers/Was ever haunted with her husbands ghost: The passion written by

a feeling pen,/And acted by a good Tragedian/She was so mooved with the sight thereof, As she cried out ... And openly confesst her husbands murder'. The author of the play is mostly listed as 'anonymous' but John Lyly, Shakespeare, Ben Jonson, Thomas Lodge, Thomas Heywood, Thomas Kyd, and the very obscure Robert Yarington, have all been mentioned as possible authors. Thomas Kyd wrote a pamphlet (not a play!) in the 1590s with a similar story at its heart, *The Murder of John Brewen*—the actual murder having occurred in 1573. For more, see Charles Dale Cannon, *A Warning for Fair Women: A Critical Edition*, Mouton and Co., The Hague, 1975, p.157.

2   The standing ovation has become a challenge for social scientists and complexity theorists because of its macro-behaviours, micro-motives and intricate social dynamics. See John H. Miller and Scott E. Page, 'The Standing Ovation Problem', *Complexity*, Vol. 9, Issue 5, June 2004, pp.8–16 (doi.org/10.1002/cplx.20033).

3   Immanuel Kant, *Critique of the Power of Judgment* (The Cambridge Edition of the Works of Immanuel Kant), Paul Guyer (ed.), Paul Guyer and Eric Matthews (transl.), Cambridge University Press, Cambridge, 2000.

4   Ibid, Editor's Introduction, p.xxxiv.

5   Ibid, §49, 5:314, p.192.

6   I.A. Richards, *Principles of Literary Criticism*, Routledge Classics, London, (1924) 2001, p.2.

7   William Wordsworth, *Wordsworth and Coleridge: Lyrical Ballads, 1798 and 1802*, Fiona Stafford (ed. and intro.), Oxford University Press, Oxford, 2013, p.98.

Thought Three

1   https://www.youtube.com/watch?v=oP3c1h8v2ZQ

2   Kurt Vonnegut, *Palm Sunday*, Random House, New York, 2010, Loc.4189. Here he goes into quite some detail and adds two more curves: the creation myth (a stepped gradual incline), and the expulsion from the Garden (a rapid decline!).

3   Though the first 'graph' of this kind I can find is in Laurence Sterne's *Tristram Shandy*, Volume IX, Chapter Four, when Corporal Trim sums up his life with an upward flourish of his cane, represented in the novel by a woodcut (that Sterne paid for himself!), a wiggly, almost vertical, black line.

4   This of course was not new news. For more context see: Robert Segal (ed. and intro.), *In Quest of the Hero*, Princeton University Press, Princeton, 1990; or also Vladimir Propp, *Morphology of the Folktale,* Preface and Introduction to the First and Second Editions, University of Austin, Austin, (1928) 1968.

5   His 2004 lecture was transcribed and can be found here: https://www.laphamsquarterly.org/arts-letters/blackboard. The short

ENDNOTES   141

video is here: https://www.youtube.com/watch?v=GOGru_4z1Vc; the full
54 minutes are here: https://www.youtube.com/watch?v=4_RUgnC1lm8
6   Kurt Vonnegut, *Bagombo Snuff Box: Uncollected Short Fiction*,
Vintage, London, 2000, pp.9–10.
7   Professor Aaker also teaches a module on 'The Power of Story':
powerofstory.stanford.edu. For the sins see: https://www.gsb.stanford.edu/
insights/jennifer-aaker-seven-deadly-sins-storytelling
8   Hayden White, 'The burden of history', *History and Theory*, 5
(1966), p.134.
9   Northrop Frye, *Anatomy of Criticism: Four Essays*, Princeton
University Press, (1957) 2000, p.140. And while he was more than happy to
discuss the collective unconscious, he figured it was itself unnecessary for
the literary critic.
10   C.G. Jung, *The Archetypes and the Collective Unconscious*, R.F.C.
Hull (transl.), Routledge, New York, 2nd Ed., 1968 (1959), p.6.
11   Regrettably, when the archetypes themselves are enumerated
and made definitive, it muddles the differences Jung asserted existed
between the archetypal form and the archetypal image; plus his
archetypes were conceived of as fluid rather than unchanging. For some
examples of recent interest see Dale M. Kushner, 'The Hero's Journey in
the time of COVID', *Psychology Today*, 30 August 2020 and 'Fathers: Heroes,
Villains, and Our Need for Archetypes', *Psychology Today*, 31 May 2018;
Michael A. Faber and John D. Mayer, 'Resonance to archetypes in media:
There's some accounting for taste', *Journal of Research in Personality*, 43 (3),
June 2009, pp.307–322; Garret Hall, 'The Jungian Psychology of Cool: Ryan
Gosling and the Repurposing of Midcentury Male Rebels', *Proceedings of
The National Conference On Undergraduate Research (NCUR)*, April 2013,
University of Wisconsin La Crosse; and Margaret Mark and Carol S.
Pearson, *The Hero and the Outlaw: Building extraordinary brands through the
power of archetypes*, McGraw-Hill, New York, 2001.
12   The University of Illinois professors asked after: food and shelter,
safety and security, social support and love, respect and pride, mastery
and self-direction, and autonomy. Ed Diener and Louis Tay, 'Needs and
Subjective Well-Being Around the World', *Journal of Personality and Social
Psychology*, American Psychological Association, 2011, Vol. 101, No. 2,
pp.354–365. Available online: https://www.apa.org/pubs/journals/releases/
psp-101-2-354.pdf or doi.org/10.1037/a0023779
13   There is one numbered list, possibly the twentieth century's
most important literary list, worth reviewing. Soviet scholar Roman
Jakobson looked to language's synchronic purpose (what it is doing at a
given time). A key founding member of what became known as Czech
and Russian Formalism, Jakobson identified the six core parts of the
communication process. Language needs: 1.) a sender, 2.) a message,
and 3.) an addressee or receiver. The message requires: 4.) a context
graspable by the addressee, and 5.) a common code (known or partial,
verbal or capable of being verbalised). Finally it entails: 6.) contact—a

physical channel and/or psychological connection between the sender and receiver. Jakobson proposed that each part determined a different linguistic functionality and that messages and meanings cannot be isolated from their context. Jakobson's work continues to be influential across phonology, poetics, philology, aphasia and semiotics, most especially in his search for the accord between phonemes, phonetic properties, a whole work, poetry in general and history in particular: 'poeticalness is not a supplementation of discourse with rhetorical adornment but a total re-evaluation of the discourse and all its components whatsoever'. See Roman Jakobson, *Language in Literature*, Krystyna Pomorska and Stephen Rudy (eds.), Belknap/Harvard University Press, Cambridge, 1987, p.93.

14   For more see Joseph Campbell, *The Hero with a Thousand Faces*, Princeton University Press, Princeton, 1949; but also Donald Palumbo, *The mono myth in American science fiction films: 28 visions of the hero's journey*, McFarland, Jefferson, 2014; and Helena Bassil-Morozow and Luke Hockley, *Jungian Film Studies: The Essential Guide*, Routledge, London, 2017. After Campbell's death his antipathy to 'Marxists', African-Americans and Jews was widely debated. For more see Brendan Gill, 'The Faces of Joseph Campbell', *The New York Review of Books*, 28 September 1989: https://www.nybooks.com/articles/1989/09/28/the-faces-of-joseph-campbell/ and the many letters in response: https://www.nybooks.com/articles/1989/11/09/joseph-campbell-an-exchange/. For more on the relationship between Campbell and George Lucas see: https://www.starwars.com/news/mythic-discovery-within-the-inner-reaches-of-outer-space-joseph-campbell-meets-george-lucas-part-i

15   Campbell's hero's journey had 17 parts in three 'acts': Act one, Departure—The Call to Adventure, Refusal of the Call, Supernatural Aid, The Crossing of the First Threshold, the Belly of the Whale; Act two, Initiation—The Road of Trials, The Meeting with the Goddess, Woman as the Temptress, Atonement with the Father/Abyss, Apotheosis, The Ultimate Boon; Act three, Return—The Refusal of the Return, The Magic Flight, Rescue from Without, The Crossing of the Return Threshold, Master of the Two Worlds, Freedom to Live. Christopher Vogler also offered eight character archetypes: Hero, Mentor, Threshold Guardian, Herald, Shapeshifter, Shadow, Ally and Trickster.

16   *Star Wars: Episode IV–A New Hope* as the hero's journey: 1. We start in a relatively ordinary world (Luke doing chores on Tatooine); 2. There is a call to adventure, the revelation of an unsuspected world, a fateful region of treasure and danger (R2D2 and the glitchy message, old Ben's place and the light sabre); 3. The quest is refused (Luke rejects the option to help the Princess in distress, despite meeting old Uncle Ben Kenobi, R2D2 and C3PO); 4. The hero accepts the call having met their mentor in a cave (Luke is goaded into action on the deaths of his aunt and uncle, he realises old Ben is more than he seems); 5a. The hero crosses the first threshold and enters the unknown (after completing some

ENDNOTES

brave trials Luke acquits himself in the bar and onboard the Millennium Falcon); 5b. They receive supernatural aid (Luke, via Obi-Wan, learns more of The Force); 5c. They receive a talisman (the light sabre); 6. In the extraordinary world the hero is tested, finds both allies and enemies (Han Solo, Chewie, the Rebel Alliance versus The Empire); 7. After facing an ordeal, the hero mishandles the situation (Alderaan is destroyed and they are caught by the Empire) crossing the second threshold; 8. The hero may retreat to a cave at their lowest ebb, though with an understanding of sacrifice (the death of Obi-Wan, Luke saw Obi-Wan submit to Darth Vader to engineer their escape); 9. The hero has a reward (the Death Star plans are delivered to the Rebels and the Princess is saved), crossing the third threshold; 10. The road back (Luke and the gang return to the Rebels, but they are being tracked, they must now take action, or all die); 11. The hero is faced by a supreme ordeal (Luke destroys the Death Star guided by Obi-Wan and the Force) and is resurrected (a new battle-hardened Luke is born); 12. Return with the elixir (Luke has brought peace to the galaxy, for now) and become the cosmic dancer (not sure though that Luke dances, or trips gaily between worlds) crossing the fourth threshold to peace and being at one-ment.

17   For more see: Derrick Parkhurst, Klinton Law, Ernst Niebur, 'Modeling the role of salience in the allocation of overt visual attention', *Vision Research*, Volume 42, Issue 1, January 2002, pp.107–123 (doi. org/10.1016/S0042-6989(01)00250-4); Jonathan Grainger, Arnaud Rey, Stéphane Dufau, 'Letter perception: from pixels to pandemonium', *Trends in Cognitive Science*, Vol. 12, Issue 10, Oct 2008, pp.381–387 (doi. org/10.1016/j.tics.2008.06.006).

18   Elly Ifantidou, 'Newspaper headlines and relevance: Ad hoc concepts in ad hoc contexts', *Journal of Pragmatics*, Vol. 41, Issue 4, April 2009, pp.699–720 (doi.org/10.1016/j.pragma.2008.10.016).

19   Walter Kintsch, 'Recognition and free recall of organized lists', *Journal of Experimental Psychology*, Vol. 78(3, Pt.1), Nov 1968, pp.481–487 (doi.org/10.1037/h0026462); Daniel M. Oppenheimer, 'The secret life of fluency' *Trends in Cognitive Science*, Vol. 12, Issue 6, 2008, pp.237–41 (doi. org/10.1016/j.tics.2008.02.014).

20   Claude Messner and Michaela Wänke, 'Unconscious information processing reduces information overload and increases product satisfaction', *Journal of Consumer Psychology*, Vol. 21, Issue 1, 2011, pp.9–13 (doi.org/10.1016/j.jcps.2010.09.010); Colin Camerer and Martin Weber, 'Recent developments in modeling preferences: Uncertainty and ambiguity', *Journal of Risk and Uncertainty*, 5, 1992, pp.325–370 (doi. org/10.1007/BF00122575).

21   This is a huge and contentious field in cognitive science. For more see Roger C. Schank and Robert P. Abelson, 'Knowledge and Memory: The Real story', in Robert S. Wyer (ed.), *Knowledge and Memory: the Real Story, Advances in Social Cognition, Vol. VIII*, Psychology Press, New York, (1995) 2014, pp.1–85.

22   *The Nātyaśāstra ascribed to Bharata-Muni*, Manmohan Ghosh (transl. and ed.), Asiatic Society of Bengal, Calcutta, 1951, pp.16–17.
23   Anne Bogart, *And then you act: Making art in an unpredictable world*, Routledge, New York, 2007, p.71.
24   David Lan has suggested that almost every single-protagonist play in the world consists of five elements: a character exists in a culture; that character is suffering; that character then does something, maybe goes on a journey, to alleviate that suffering; they encounter obstacles; in the end, either they, or we, learn something. As you will notice, the actual 'play' part is really only included in steps three, four and five.
25   Suzan-Lori Parks, 'Elements of Style', in *The America Play and Other Works*, Theatre Communications Group, New York, 1994, pp.12–15.
26   Scientists, as Vonnegut hoped they would, put stories into computers, and they came up with the number six—six common stories: rise (rags to riches), fall (riches to rags), man in hole (fall then rise), Icarus (rise then fall), Cinderella (rise, fall, rise) and Oedipus (fall, rise, fall). The University of Vermont's Computational Lab ran 1,737 books from Project Gutenberg (all in English, some in translation) through a complicated series of programs and following some tough maths in order to chart the emotional journeys of the main character. Their methodology is fascinating and they go into great depth to explain their working, sources and formulae. For more see: Andrew J. Reagan, Lewis Mitchell, Dilan Kiley, Christopher M. Danforth and Peter Sheridan Dodds, 'The emotional arcs of stories are dominated by six basic shapes', *EPJ Data Science*, Vol. 5:31, 2016, pp.1–12, and appendices A–H, pp.S1–S103. It is all available free online: https://epjdatascience.springeropen.com/articles/10.1140/epjds/s13688-016-0093-1

Thought Four

1   For a terrific introduction see Lilla Maria Crisafulli and Fabio Liberto, *The Romantic Stage: A Many Sided Mirror*, DQR Studies in Literature, Vol. 55, Brill, Leiden, 2015.
2   For more on this in practice see Jane Armstrong, *The Arden Shakespeare Miscellany*, Bloomsbury, London, 2011, Chapter VII, p.173; and also Margreta de Grazia and Peter Stallybrass, 'The Materiality of the Shakespearean Text', *Shakespeare Quarterly*, Vol. 44, No. 3, 1993, pp.255–283.
3   Legendary British actress Sarah Siddons quoted in Catherine B. Burroughs, *Closet Stages: Joanna Baillie and the Theater Theory of British Romantic Women Writers*, University of Pennsylvania Press, Bloomington, 1997, p.54.
4   Frederick Garber, 'Self, Society, Value, and the Romantic Hero', *Comparative Literature*, Vol. 19, No. 4, Autumn, 1967, pp.321–333.
5   August Wilhelm von Schlegel, *Lectures on dramatic art and literature*, John Black (transl.), Rev. A.J.W. Morrison (ed.), George Bell & Sons, London, 1889, Lecture XXV, p.407.

ENDNOTES

6   Williams from his *Where I Live: Selected Essays*, Christine R. Day (intro. and ed.) and Bob Woods (ed.), A New Directions Book, New York, 1978, p.72, an article written for the *New York Herald Tribune* (April 17, 1955) in response to a review of *Cat on a Hot Tin Roof* accusing him of 'evasion' with respect to certain character questions, most especially about Brick; see also William Storm, *Dramaturgy and Dramatic Character: A Long View*, Cambridge University Press, Cambridge, 2016, p.51.

7   Elinor Fuchs, 'E.F.'s Visit to a Small Planet: Some Questions to ask a Play', *Theatre*, 34.2, 2004, pp.5–9; also reprinted in Magda Romanska (ed.), *The Routledge Companion to Dramaturgy*, Routledge, Abingdon, 2014, Part VII, Essay 68.

8   Though it is a Greek story it has come down to us in Latin courtesy of Roman-North African writer Apuleius. As a result it is often referred to as the story of 'Cupid and Psyche', though the Greeks called them Aphrodite, Eros and Psyche, and the Romans called them Venus, Cupid and Anima. For a recent rendering see Stephen Fry, *Mythos*, Penguin, London, 2017, pp.157–186.

9   And, for fun, and to get a sense of the myth's valency, just try replacing the character names Cupid and Psyche with the words 'love' and 'soul'—love abandoned soul when she saw him in the light, soul endured miserable trials in pursuit of love etc.

10   Gabriel Mingard quoted in Fernando Vidal, *The Science of the Soul: The Early Modern Origins of Psychology*, Saskia Brown (transl.), University of Chicago Press, Chicago, 2011, p.1.

11   Quoted in Vidal, *Science of the Soul*, p.97. Though Voltaire was very much a fan of Locke and the philosophical approach to studying the soul over an empirical approach.

12   The word 'character' itself derives from the Greek 'kharekter', a stamping tool (into wax, leather etc.). It was extended, metaphorically, to mean a distinctive individual feature in Hellenistic times. It was adopted into English in the 17th century to mean the sum of all qualities that defines a person; and at about the same time as it applies to a person in a play, poem or book.

13   The philosopher Michel Foucault has argued that medicalisation of social discourse, or rather, the embedding of social and economic conditions by medical testing in the body through new notions of 'wellness' and 'normalcy', began in 1778 with the commencement of the *Société Royale de Médecine* and modern medicine's promise of the general improvement, or the scientific curing, of society. For more see his *The Birth of the Clinic: An Archaeology of Medical Perception*, Routledge, Abingdon, 2003 (1963 in France, first English publication 1973). His controversial revisionist view of medical history has received much attention; for an assessment see Colin Jones and Roy Porter (eds.), *Reassessing Foucault: Power, medicine and the body*, Routledge, Abingdon, 1994.

14   Stephen Briers, *Psychobabble: Exploding the myths of the self-help generation*, Pearson, London, 2012, p.2.

15   The observation on Wundt's lectures is from American psychologist Frank Angell who studied under Wundt and set up experimental psychology labs at Cornell (1891) and Stanford (1892); 'Wilhelm Wundt', *American Journal of Psychology*, Vol. 32, 1921, pp.161–178; for more on other labs see John D. Hogan and Thomas P. Vaccaro, 'International Perspectives on the History of Psychology', in Michael J. Stevens and Uwe P. Gielen (eds.), *Towards a Global Psychology: Theory, Research, Intervention and Pedagogy*, Lawrence Erlbaum Associates, New Jersey, 2007, pp.41–42.

16   See Roy Porter, *Blood and Guts: A Short History of Medicine*, Penguin, 2003, Chapter Four especially; Gary Hatfield, 'Remaking the Science of Mind: Psychology as Natural Science', in Christopher Fox, Roy Porter and Robert Wokler (eds.), *Inventing Human Science: Eighteenth Century Domains*, University of California Press, Berkeley, 1995, pp.184–231; Nikolas Rose, *Governing the Soul*, 1989; and also Mark S. Micale and Roy Porter (eds.), *Discovering the history of Psychiatry*, Oxford University Press, Oxford, 1994.

17   Michel Foucault, *Discipline and Punish: the birth of the prison*, Vintage Books, New York, 1979, p.191.

18   For more on the shift in understanding of the gaze see Daniel Pick, 'Stories of the Eye', in Roy Porter (ed.), op-cit, (1997), pp.186–199. And of course in Foucault, *The Birth of the Clinic*, (1963), passim.

19   See Carole Spitzack, 'Foucault's Political Body in Medical Praxis', in Drew Leder (ed.), *The Body in medical thought and praxis*, Philosophy and Medicine Vol. 43, Kluwer Academic Publishers, The Netherlands, 1992, pp.51–68.

20   Gilles Deleuze, *Foucault*, Seán Hand (transl. and ed.), Continuum, London, 1988, p.50.

21   Nikolas Rose, *Inventing our Selves: Psychology, Power and Personhood*, Cambridge University Press, Cambridge, 1998, p.81.

22   Paul Ricoeur, *Freud and Philosophy: An Essay on Interpretation*, Denis Savage (transl.), Yale University Press, New Haven, 1970.

23   Zola quoted in Maggie Gale and John Deenedy (eds.), *Routledge Drama Anthology*, Routledge, Abingdon, 2020, p.135.

24   Zola quoted in Toby Cole, *Playwrights on Playwriting*, Cooper Square Press, New York, 2001, p.6.

25   Zola quoted in Gale and Deenedy (eds.), *Routledge Drama Anthology*, 2020, pp.134–135.

26   This is taken from Benedetti's translation of Stanislavsky's Russian version, not the American version of 1924. See Stanislavski, *My Life in Art*, Jean Benedetti (transl.), Routledge, Abingdon, 2008, p.93. The same passage appears, in a slightly amended version, in the 1924 J.J. Robbins translation, *My Life in Art* (1959), p.155.

27   Stanislavsky, *My Life in Art* (1959), pp.462–463.

ENDNOTES

28   Stanislavsky, *My Life in Art* (1959), p.483.
29   Each came to adopt an increasing focus on realism, naturalism,
then on Stanislavsky's system over the first 30 years of the 20th century.
For more see: Peter Zazzali, *Acting in the Academy: The history of Professional
Actor Training in US Higher Education*, Routledge, Abingdon, 2016; Robert
Leach, *An Illustrated History of British Theatre and Performance: Volume II—
From the Industrial Revolution to the Digital Age*, Routledge, Abingdon, 2019.

Thought Five

1   All quotations from Lessing are taken from the standard,
incomplete, but first English translation first published c.1879,
G.E. Lessing, *Hamburg Dramaturgy*, Helen Zimmern (transl.), Dover
Publications, New York, 1962. In Essays 101–104.
2   Lessing, *Hamburg Dramaturgy*, Preface.
3   Much has been written on the Enlightenment, der Aufklärung,
'the Age of Reason', with it described as a great leap forward for
civilisation, liberty and the rational autonomous subject; and that it
accompanied a logarithmic growth in Western prosperity. More recently
however it has come under intense criticism, most particularly in the
20th century for resulting in, justifying, or allowing, colonialism, slavery,
racism, sexism and genocide. A classic text in its favour is Isaiah Berlin's
mid-century collection of documents and his very influential introduction
in *The Age of Enlightenment: The Eighteenth Century Philosophers*, Penguin,
New York, 1956. More recently psychologist Steven Pinker has written
in favour of the Enlightenment and its utopian championing of reason
and liberal democracy, in his opinion, the twin great bulwarks against
the forces of anti-civilisation. For the counter claims see: Adorno and
Horkheimer, *Dialectic of Enlightenment*, 1944, John Cumming (transl.),
Verso, 1979; Benjamin's seventh thesis on the philosophy of history in
Illuminations, Arendt (ed.) Zohn (transl.) Fontana, 1973; works by Foucault,
Derrida and Sarah Kofman, and Zygmunt Bauman, *Modernity and the
Holocaust*, Polity Press, Cambridge, 1989; and from the 19th century see
Vico or Nietzsche. In 2018 journalist Jamelle Bouie wrote an article for
slate.com, 'The Enlightenment's Dark Side: How the Enlightenment created
modern race thinking and why we should confront it' June 5 2018: https://
slate.com/news-and-politics/2018/06/taking-the-enlightenment-seriously-
requires-talking-about-race.html
4   Lessing, Essays 101–104.
5   The term itself had been used twice previously by
contemporaries and it is likely that Lessing had copies of those books,
both of them of Italian origin. The first was the second edition of Lione
Allaci's *La Drammaturgia*, a list of every Italian musical drama presented
up to 1755. Lessing's own design though far exceeded a catalogue or
almanac (and indeed in France in the 1740s and 50s it was no uncommon
practice to print theatrical catalogues, *histoires* and *dictionnaires*). The

other book that employed the compound word was Ottaviano Diodati's
12-volume *Biblioteca teatrale italiano* (published 1762–5), which was a
collection of recent Italian plays but which also included chapters in verse
'*per servire di tratto completo di Drammaturgia*' (to serve the complete pieces/
expanse/section of the Dramaturgy) that included discussion of the art of
dramatic representation, scene changes, modes of recitation, declamation
and gesture. Discussion and analysis of the '*tratto completo*' of the drama
was exactly what Lessing had in mind. That word, '*drammaturgia*', had
gone from ancient Greek into Italian and then into French as a result
of Allaci's book, and while Diderot did not use it, progressive French
encyclopedist, critic and playwright Jean-Francois Marmontel (1723–1799)
did, adopting '*dramaturge*' as the French word for a writer of plays.
6   See J.W. Eaton,'Johann Elias Schlegel in Denmark', *The Modern
Language Review*, Vol. 23, No. 1, 1928), pp. 28–42 (doi.org/10.2307/3713968),
and his *The German influence in Danish Literature in the eighteenth century:
The German circle in Copenhagen 1750–1770*, Cambridge University
Press, Cambridge, 1929, pp. 46–7; and also George W. Brandt and Wiebe
Hogendoorn, *German and Dutch Theatre 1600–1848*, Cambridge University
Press, Cambridge, 1993, p.195.
7   From Essay 95, p.251. The Latin means, literally, 'fermenting of
knowledge'. Hannah Arendt, who won the Lessing Prize in 1959, wrote an
essay in 1955 on the solace this phrase provided her, most particularly that
Lessing was a partisan for a world 'capable of supporting, sustaining and
stimulating multiple and conflicting voices and strivings'. Kimberley F.
Curtis commented in 1997 that for Arendt the phrase suggested 'thoughts
designed both to strengthen the position of opinions so embattled that
their very existence as an angle on the world was at risk' and 'thoughts
that would stimulate the emergence of new options' referring to Lessing
as 'a polemicist for the multidimensionality of the world of discourse'.
From Kimberley F. Curtis, 'Aesthetic Foundations of Democratic Politics in
the work of Hannah Arendt' in Craig Calhoun and John McGowan (eds.),
Hannah Arendt and the Meaning of Politics, Contradictions of Modernity
Vol.6, University of Minnesota Press, Minneapolis, 1997, pp.31–2.
8   In a digression inside a digression, Essays 60-68 summarise
a Spanish play that was similar, but not the same, as the Corneille play
under discussion (written by Thomas Corneille, the far less well-known
younger brother of legendary playwright Pierre Corneille) and which
are not even included in the standard translation! The Essays jump from
No.59 to 69, with but a rather droll note: '[Lessing now devotes many
pages to a detailed account of an old and anonymous Spanish play dealing
with the subject of Essex.]' The Essays have now been translated and are
included in the new translation. See Wendy Arons and Sara Figal (transl),
Natalya Baldyga (ed.), *The Hamburg Dramaturgy by G.E. Lessing: A New and
Complete Annotated English Translation*, Routledge, New York, 2019.
9   Essay 15.
10   Essay 50.

ENDNOTES

11   Essays 101–104.

12   This list is drawn from Mary Luckhurst in her book *Dramaturgy: A revolution in theatre*, Cambridge University Press, 2006, p.37: *The Vienna Dramaturgy* (1775), *The Mannheim Dramaturgy* (1779), *Didascalia or Reflections on Dramaturgy* (1796), *The New Hamburg Dramaturgy* (1791), Schink *Dramaturgy Fragments* (1781), and Adolph von Knigge *Dramaturgical Papers* (1789).

13   Bertolt Brecht, *The Messingkauf Dialogues*, John Willett (transl.), Methuen, London, 1965, p.10. See also *Brecht on Performance: Messingkauf and Modelbooks*, Tom Kuhn, Steve Giles and Marc Silberman (eds.), Bloomsbury Methuen, London, 2014.

14   See for instance: Peter Hay, 'American Dramaturgy: A Critical Re-Appraisal', *Performing Arts Journal*, Vol. 7, No. 3 (1983), pp.7–24; Marianne van Kerkhoven, 'Introduction to "on Dramaturgy"', *Theaterschrift*, No.5–6, 1994, pp.8–34 and 'Looking without pencil in the hand', *Theaterschrift*, No.5–6, 1994, pp.142–4; Susan S. Jonas, Geoffrey S. Proehl and Michael Lupo (eds.), *Dramaturgy in American Theatre: A Source Book*, Cengage Learning, 1996; Mary Luckhurst, *Dramaturgy: A Revolution in Theatre*, Cambridge University Press, Cambridge, 2006; Cathy Turner, Synne Behrndt, *Dramaturgy and Performance*, Palgrave Macmillan, London 2nd Ed, 2016; Eugenio Barba, *On directing and dramaturgy: burning the house*, Judy Barba (transl.), Routledge, London, 2010; Michael Mark Chemers, *Ghost Light: An Introductory Handbook for Dramaturgy*, Southern Illinois University Press, Carbondale, 2010; Peter Eckersall, Melanie Beddie, Paul Monaghan (eds.), *Dramaturgies: new theatres for the 21st century: document and debates from Dramaturgies #4*, Dramaturgies Project, Melbourne, 2011; Katalin Trencsényi and Bernadette Cochrane (eds), *New Dramaturgy: International Perspectives on Theory and Practice*, Bloomsbury Publishing, London, 2014; Katalin Trencsényi, *Dramaturgy in the Making: A User's Guide for Theatre Practitioners*, Bloomsbury Publishing, London, 2015; Magda Romanska (ed.), *The Routledge Companion to Dramaturgy*, Routledge, London, 2015; Pil Hansen and Darcey Callison (eds.), *Dance Dramaturgy: Modes of Agency, Awareness and Engagement*, Palgrave Macmillan, London, 2015; Katherine Profeta, *Dramaturgy in Motion: At work on dance and movement performance*, The University of Wisconsin Press, Madison, 2015; Alyson Campbell and Stephen Farrier (eds.), *Queer Dramaturgies: International Perspectives on Where Performance Leads Queer*, Palgrave Macmillan, London, 2016; Theresa Lang, *Essential Dramaturgy: The Mindset and Skillset*, Routledge, London, 2017; Fiona Graham, *Performing dramaturgy*, Playmarket, Wellington, 2017; Tore Vagn Lid, *Reflexive Dramaturgy: Etudes for the (performing) arts in a time of change*, Cappelen Damm Akademisk, Oslo, 2018; and Mark Bly, *New Dramaturgies: Strategies and Exercises for 21st Century Playwriting*, Routledge, London, 2019. See also the very useful online Dramaturgy Database compiled by Utrecht University's Digital Humanities Lab (https://dramaturgydatabase.hum.uu.nl/about/).

15   List taken from Bojana Kunst, 'The Economy of Proximity: Dramaturgical Work in Contemporary Dance', *Performance Research*, 14:3, 2009, pp.81–88.

16   See Theresa Lang, *Essential Dramaturgy*, 2017, p.7.

17   See: https://www.dramaturgy.co.uk/single-post/keep-asking-questions

18   From *The Theatre Times*, 5 September, 2016: https://thetheatretimes.com/mark-bly-in-conversation-with-katalin-trencsenyi-questioning-spirit-dramaturgy-in-america/

19   Michael Mark Chemers, *Ghost Light*, 2010, p.4.

20   Ivan D. Illich, *Tools for Conviviality*, Calder and Boyars, London, 1973; Donna J. Haraway, *Staying with the Trouble: Making Kin in the Chthulucene*, Duke University Press, Durham, 2016.

21   Jane Bennett, *Vibrant Matter: A political ecology of things*, Duke University Press, Durham, 2010, p.4.

22   Thomas Ollive Abbott (ed.), *Collected Works of Edgar Allan Poe*, Harvard University Press, Vol.3, 1978, p.1113. See also Aldo Corcella, 'A Source for Poe's "Marginalia"', *The Edgar Allan Poe Review*, Vol. 18, No. 2, 2017, pp. 193–208. See also: https://www.brainpickings.org/2013/09/17/edgar-allan-poe-marginalia/ and https://www.newyorker.com/books/page-turner/the-marginal-obsession-with-marginalia

Thought Six

1   For a useful primer see: Robert Burton, 'Where Science and Story Meet', in *Nautilus*, 22 April, 2013, https://nautil.us/issue/0/the-story-of-nautilus/where-science-and-story-meet; see also his *A Skeptic's Guide to the Mind: What Neuroscience Can and Cannot Tell Us About Ourselves*, St Martin's Press, New York, 2014.

2   Charles Duhigg, *The Power of Habit: Why we do what we do in life and business*, Random House, London, 2012.

3   See Cort A Pederson and Arthur J. Prange Jr, 'Induction of maternal behavior in virgin rats after intracerebroventricular administration of oxytocin', *Proceedings of the National Academy of Sciences of the USA*, December 1979: https://www.pnas.org/content/76/12/6661

4   I am indebted to this article for mention of marketing with story as a funnel: Giovanni René Rodriguez, 'This is your Brain on Storytelling; The Chemistry of Modern Communication', Forbes, 21 July 2017: https://www.forbes.com/sites/giovannirodriguez/2017/07/21/this-is-your-brain-on-storytelling-the-chemistry-of-modern-communication/?sh=48e803a9c865

5   Jorge A. Barraza, J. A. and Paul J. Zak, 'Empathy toward strangers triggers oxytocin release and subsequent generosity', *Annals of the New York Academy of Sciences*, Vol. 1167 Issue 1, 2009, pp.182–189. A digital version can be found here: http://www.neuroeconomicstudies.org/publications

6   Paul Zak's TED Talk has been flagged on the TED site as

ENDNOTES

having been challenged, with its own tab just for criticism and updates. https://www.ted.com/pages/criticism-updates-paul-zak. For dissenting views see: https://www.scientificamerican.com/article/fact-or-fiction-oxytocin-is-the-love-hormone/ and also https://www.theatlantic.com/science/archive/2015/11/the-weak-science-of-the-wrongly-named-moral-molecule/415581/

7   For more see studies by Ernst Fehr, Gideon Nave, Michael McCullough and Larry Young. See also, from 2015: https://www.nature.com/news/neuroscience-the-hard-science-of-oxytocin-1.17813 and https://www.theatlantic.com/science/archive/2015/11/the-weak-science-of-the-wrongly-named-moral-molecule/415581/

8   Suzana Herculano-Houzel, *The Human Advantage: A New Understanding of How Our Brain became Remarkable*, The MIT Press, Cambridge MA, 2016.

9   Herculano-Houzel argues that, on reviewing the literature, there was no source for this number plucked from the air, possibly as a result of some guesswork and wishful thinking via neurostereology. For a series of 10 articles on neurostereology, its methodological challenges and new solutions see: Bente Pakkenberg, Mikkel Vestergaard Olesen, Sanne Simone Kaalund and Karl-Anton Dorph-Petersen (eds.), in a recent issue of the journal *Frontiers in Neuroanatomy*, Vol.13, 2019 (doi.org/10.3389/fnana.2019.00042).

10   Except in a note on p.264. For more on birds see: Nathan Emery, *Bird Brain: An Exploration of Avian Intelligence*, Princeton University Press, Princeton, 2016.

11   Positron Emission Tomography (PET) and its earlier iteration, CT or Computed Tomography, invented in 1971; functional Magnetic Resonance Imaging (fMRI) first developed in this way from the late 1980s into the early 1990s; and also Electroencephalography (EEG); Electrocorticography (ECoG); Magnetoencephalography (MEG); and, most recently, optical imaging with Near-Infrared Spectroscopy (NIRS).

12   Phineas Gage was an American railway worker who survived an explosion in which an iron rod was driven through his head. It destroyed most of his frontal lobe, causing profound character changes. He lived for 12 years subsequent to the accident. For more on history see Andrew P. Wickens, *A History of the Brain: From Stone Age surgery to modern neuroscience*, Psychology Press, London, 2014; Stanley Finger, *Origins of Neuroscience: A History of Explorations into Brain Function*, Oxford University Press, Oxford, 1994; Mitchell Glickstein, *Neuroscience: A Historical Introduction*, The MIT Press, Cambridge MA, 2014; For more on Gage see Malcolm Macmillan, *An Odd Kind of Fame: Stories of Phineas Gage*, THE MIT Press, Cambridge MA, 2002.

13   Wilder Penfield and Theodore Rasmussen, *The Cerebral Cortex of Man*, Macmillan, New York, 1950. For the Homunculus, as he called it, see Figures 10, 17 and 22, pp.25, 44 and 57. See also William Feindel and Richard Leblanc, *The Wounded Brain Healed: The Golden Age of the*

Montreal Neurological Institute, 1934–1984, McGill-Queen's University Press, Kingston, 2016 or Rodolfo R. Llinás, *I of the Vortex: From Neurons to Self*, Bedford Book MIT Press, Cambridge MA, 2002, pp.115–122.

14   Penfield quoted in his Royal Society obituary by J.C. Eccles, 1978, p.498: https://royalsocietypublishing.org/doi/pdf/10.1098/rsbm.1978.0015

15   For a withering classic critique of biological determinism see Stephen Jay Gould's, *The Mismeasure of Man*, Revised and Expanded, W.W. Norton, New York, (1981) 2006.

16   The world's fastest supercomputer, Japan's Fugaku (ranked best in the world across four different measures) took six years of engineering and 1,200 co-design meetings between software and hardware engineers to construct, consists of 432 x 2m high racks, occupies an entire floor of the RIKEN Center for Computational Studies in Kobe, is the computational equivalent of 20 million smartphones, requires an intricate underfloor cooling system (another storey!), is entirely non-portable, cost about US$1billion and while energy efficient, still uses 30 megawatts of energy to run (enough to power, very roughly 1,000 average homes). The human brain weighs 1.5kg, is the size of a couple of fists, runs well at room temperature, we walk around with it everywhere, and though now an order of magnitude behind Fugaku (2 eFLOPS plays 1 pFLOPS) it only uses 15 watts of energy, max. Just in the past decade have computers jumped from 1 pFLOPS to 442 pFLOPS, with Fugaku, by some measures, also achieving 2 exaFLOPS. Computer performance is measured in kiloFLOPS (10^3), mega [106], giga [109], tera [1012], peta [1015], exa [1018], zetta and yotta. These numbers feel ultimately abstract but you can visualise one million US dollar bills stacked on top of one another, and they are roughly the height of a chair; a billion dollar bills equates roughly to one kilometre high, or just a bit higher than the world's tallest building; and a trillion dollar bills would be over 1,000km out into the atmosphere, or two and a half times further away than the International Space Station (and well past the Kármán line, but nowhere near the Moon, which is just over 380,000kms away). And FLOPS? This is a computing term, an acronym for Floating Point Operations Per Second. Floating Point maths allows for numbers to be represented with accuracy whether mammoth or tiny, useful for astrophysicists and computer chip designers, though mostly used in computer programming. The 'floating' point is the decimal (or radix or binary) point, as it can be moved and the number still retains its meaning, as long as the operation itself is explained, currently the IEEE 754 Standard. For instance you can represent the first 33 digits of π (pi) as: 11001001 00001111 11011010 10100010 0.

17   George Zarkadakis, *In our own Image: Will artificial intelligence save or destroy us?* Ebury Press, London, 2015.

18   For a less optimistic view of the harnessing of brains and machines, note well (yes, there is a 2009 TED Talk) the developing story of scientist Henry Markram and the waste of $1.3 billion, see: https://www.

scientificamerican.com/article/why-the-human-brain-project-went-wrong-and-how-to-fix-it/

19   The Darwin quotation is from the last paragraph of *On the Origin of Species*; and the Warsan Shire quote is from her poem '(The Prayer)'. Here are some other of Shire's incredible images: 'I can make the blood run back up my nose, ants rushing into a hole. / We grow into smaller bodies ...' or 'Apathy is the same as war, /it all kills you, she says. / Slow like cancer in the breast / or fast like a machete in the neck'.

20   Iain McGilchrist, *The Master and His Emissary: The Divided Brain and the making of the Western World*, New Expanded Edition, Yale University Press, New Haven, (2009) 2018, pp.428–429.

21   Sue Woolfe, *The Mystery of the Cleaning Lady: A Writer Looks at Creativity and Neuroscience*, UWA Press, Perth, 2007. See also: Kate Grenville and Sue Woolfe, *Making Stories: How Ten Australian Novels Were Written*, Allen and Unwin, 2001.

22   Christopher David Stevens, 'Crooked paths to insight: the pragmatics of loose and tight construing', Doctor of Philosophy thesis, Department of Psychology, University of Wollongong, 1999, available online: https://ro.uow.edu.au/cgi/viewcontent.cgi?article=2654&context=theses

23   This was a phrase employed by a colleague of hers, critic R.P. Blackmur, writing about Henry James. For more on Langer see her *Feeling and Form* (1953) or *Mind: An Essay on Human Feeling*, especially Volume 2 (1972); or Adrienne Dengerink Chaplin, *The Philosophy of Susanne Langer: Embodied Meaning in Logic, Art and Feeling*, Bloomsbury, London, 2019. For more on embodied cognition there are three key reference works: George Lakoff and Mark Johnson, *Metaphors We Live By* (1980), Francisco Varela, Evan Thompson, and Eleanor Rosch, *The Embodied Mind* (1991); and Andy Clark, *Being There: Putting Mind, World, and Body Back Together* (1997). And for Damasio see 'The somatic marker hypothesis and the possible functions of the prefrontal cortex', *Philosophical Transaction: Biological Sciences*, Vol. 351, pp.1413–1420 and *Descartes' Error: Emotion, Reason, and the Human Brain*, Putnam Publishing, New York, 1994.

24   Their key papers are gathered here: Kahneman, Paul Slovic and Tversky (eds.), *Judgement Under Uncertainty: Heuristics and Biases*, Cambridge University Press, Cambridge, 1982; see also Thomas Gilovich, Dale Griffin and Daniel Kahneman, *Heuristics and Biases: The Psychology of Intuitive Judgement*, Cambridge University Press, Cambridge, 2002.

25   A recollected Tversky quote in Michael Lewis, *The Undoing Project: A friendship that changed the world*, Allen Lane, London, 2017.

26   https://www.theguardian.com/books/2015/jul/18/daniel-kahneman-books-interview I regret that I have got this far, speaking of overconfidence, and not yet begun to convey the impact of recent studies on other minds. With recent developments in neuroscience and theory of mind (and I have barely scratched the surface, just ask Daniel Dennett, John Searle, Jerry Fodor, V.S. Ramachandran, Norman Doidge or Kathleen

Akins) the past 70 years has also seen an increasing number of scientific studies examining animals as sentient agents, creatures that act with intelligence and character. For more on this see Thomas Nagel, Mary Midgley, Marian Stamp Dawkins, Susan Hurley and Matthew Nudds, Eric Kandel, Frans de Waal, Alison Hawthorne Deming, Peter Godfrey-Smith, Robert Sapolsky, Jaak Panksepp, Tim Flannery, Oliver Sacks and Peter Singer. Then there is Peter Wohlleben and the intelligence of trees.

27   There is much literature on each of these artists, and on the possible intersection of their life and their work and their illnesses. Here is just one article on Woolf in particular, debunking a number of mischaracterisations of her and her illness, something she described as her 'eccentric and remarkable nervous system': Susan M. Kenney and Edwin J. Kenney, Jr. 'Virginia Woolf and the Art of Madness', *The Massachusetts Review*, Vol. 23, No. 1, 1982, pp. 161–185.

28   The phrase is from the US Heritage Foundation in an article about eliminating government arts support: https://www.heritage.org/ report/ten-good-reasons-eliminate-funding-the-national-endowment-orthe-arts; for similar arguments for and against arts funding, see: https:// www.themonthly.com.au/issue/2016/october/1475244000/alison-croggon/ culture-crisis#mtr

29   For a start see: Andreas Fink, 'Creativity and schizotypy from the neuroscience perspective', *Cognitive, Affective and Behavioural Neuroscience*, 2014, pp.378–87; but also, here is a less alarming sounding summary article by Christine Mohr and Gordon Claridge 'Schizotypy—Do Not Worry, It Is Not All Worrisome', *Schizophrenia Bulletin*, Vol.41, Issue suppl 2, 2015, pp.S436–S443.

30   The webinar was posted 23 March, 2020: https://www.brainfacts. org/neuroscience-in-society/the-arts-and-the-brain/2020/the-artistic-brain--a-neuroaesthetics-approach-to-health,-well-being-and-learning--02212020

31   The latter term is a rather perjorative, negative term used in 1867 by a Boston librarian that includes works as diverse as memoir, history, documentary, verité, literary journalism, biography, dictionaries, most academic publishing and more. For a fascinating study into US books sales see: Burcu Yucesoy, Xindi Wang, Junmin Huang, and Albert László Barabási, 'Success in books: a big data approach to bestsellers,' *EPJ Data Science*, 7, 7, 2018, and https://doi.org/10.1140/epjds/s13688-018-0135-y

32   Maja Djikic, Keith Oatley, and Mihnea C. Moldoveanu, 'Opening the Closed Mind: The Effect of Exposure to Literature on the Need for Closure', *Creativity Research Journal*, 25(2), 2013, pp.149–154. See also, on narratology, Dorrit Cohn, 'Fictional versus Historical Lives: Borderlines and Borderline Cases', *The Journal of Narrative Technique*, 19(1), 1989, pp.3–24, and her *The Distinction of Fiction*, The Johns Hopkins Press, Baltimore, 1999.

33   The work of Oatley and Mar on this is extensive. See, as an example: Raymond A. Mar, and Keith Oatley, 'The Function of Fiction is the Abstraction and Simulation of Social Experience', *Perspectives*

ENDNOTES   155

on Psychological Science, 3(3), pp.173–192 (doi.org/10.1111/j.1745-
6924.2008.00073.x); or Keith Oatley, 'Fiction: Simulation of social worlds',
Trends in cognitive sciences, Vol.20, No.8, 2016, pp.618–628.
34   Thomas Browne, *Hydriotaphia, Urne-Buriall*, Chapter V, in *The
Voyce of the World: Selected Writings of Sir Thomas Browne*, Geoffrey Keynes
(ed.), The Folio Society, London, 2007, p.157.
35   Thomas Browne, *Religio Medici*, Part One, Section 36, *Ibid*, p.43.
36   Thomas Browne, *Hydriotaphia*, Ch.IV, p.149.
37   Thomas Browne, *Religio Medici*, Part One, Section 12, p.15.
38   Thomas Browne, *Religio Medici*, Part One, Sections 12 and 13,
pp.15–16.

Thought Seven

1   Nganyinytja, a senior Pitjantjatjara woman, quoted in Diana
James, 'Kinship with Country: Acts of Translation in the Cross-Cultural
Performance Space, a Case Study on the Anangu Pitjantjatjara Lands of
Central Australia', PhD thesis, Australian National University, Canberra,
p.272. The thesis is available online: https://press-files.anu.edu.au/
downloads/press/p319821/html/ch02.xhtml?referer=&page=10
2   The life of British Vice Admiral Robert FitzRoy comes to mind.
A skilled seaman, he was captain of the Beagle, twice traveling with
Darwin around the world. He was also a pioneer of the sharing of weather
information to protect life and shipping and coined the phrase 'weather
forecast'. He took his own life when not yet 60, with few believing that the
weather could be predicted systematically.
3   Paula Findlen, 'Jokes of Nature and Jokes of Knowledge: The
Playfulness of Scientific Discourse in Early Modern Europe', *Renaissance
Quarterly*, 43, 1990, pp.292–331.
4   For more see: Rhodri Lewis, 'Shakespeare's Clouds and the
Image Made by Chance', *Essays in Criticism*, Vol.LXII, No.1, 2012, pp.1–
24 (doi.org/10.1093/escrit/cgr026).
5   The word 'dislimns' is arcane and Latinate—relating in this sense
to visual art and over-painting something, removing its outline—but it
is also a pun, dis-limb, and may relate, in a medieval understanding, to
clouds being influenced by fire and air, like Antony and Cleopatra's love. It
derives from the word to illuminate (*luminare*), and on the edge (*liminal*)—
though in this negative sense it can mean to 'becloud' or obscure. It may
have been coined by Shakespeare. And here 'rack' refers to the high cirrus
clouds (as also used in *The Tempest*, Act IV, sc. 1, from line 138—'Our revels
now are ended/ ... Are melted into air ... / shall dissolve / ... Leave not a
rack behind').
6   This was a minor work, part of something larger that Descartes
initially suppressed, on hearing of what happened to Galileo. For
more see: Lucian Petrescu, 'Cartesian Meteors and Scholastic Meteors:

Descartes against the School in 1637', *Journal of the History of* Ideas 76, 2015, pp.1–18.

7   For more see: Laurence J. Lafleur, 'Descartes, Father of Modern Meteorology', *Bulletin of the American Meteorological Society*, Vol. 31, No. 4, 1950, pp.138–140.

8   Quoted in 'Descartes' Method', *Stanford Encyclopedia of Philosophy*, 3 June 2020, available online: https://plato.stanford.edu/entries/descartes-method/#MethMeteDeduCausRain

9   For more see Richard Hamblyn, *The Invention of Clouds: How an Amateur Meteorologist forged the Language of the Skies*, Picador, London, 2001.

10   David Acheson, *The Calculus Story: A Mathematical Adventure*, Oxford University Press, 2017, pp.70–71.

11   A. Rupert Hall, 'Newton versus Leibniz: from geometry to metaphysics', in *The Cambridge Companion to Newton*, edited by I. Bernard Cohen and George E. Smith, Cambridge University Press, 2002, pp.431–454; Domenico Bertoloni Meli, *Equivalence and Priority: Newton versus Leibniz*, Oxford University Press, 1993; and also in pop science form, Jason Socrates Bardi, *The Calculus Wars: Newton, Leibniz, and the Greatest Mathematical Clash of All Time*, Basic Books, New York, 2007.

12   For more see Graham Farmelo, *The Strangest Man: The Hidden Life of Paul Dirac, Quantum Genius*, Faber and Faber, London, 2009, p.169 and also Steven Strogatz, *Infinite Powers: The Story of Calculus, The Language of the Universe*, Atlantic Books, London, 2019, pp.338–9. The Dirac equation itself looks like this: $iɣ.δψ=mψ$ or $(ið-m)ψ=0$. The first equation appears on his commemorative stone in Westminster Abbey, the latter is a way of expressing it using 'natural units'. Dirac later said that the theory was built from physical concepts and 'cannot be explained in words at all' or 'like a blind man seeing a snowflake. One touch and it's gone'. As to poetry, and a corrective worth remembering, Dirac was broadly intolerant. On finding that Robert Oppenheimer both read and wrote poetry he commented to him: 'In science, you want to say something nobody knew before, in words everyone can understand. In poetry, you are bound to say something that everybody knows already in words nobody can understand.'

13   A Royal McBee LGP-30, dense with wires and vacuum tubes.

14   Edward Lorenz, 'Deterministic Non-Periodic Flow', *Journal of the Atmospheric Science*, Vol.20, 1963, p.132. Available online: https://www.astro.puc.cl/~rparra/tools/PAPERS/lorenz1962.pdf

15   *Havana*, the movie, was written by Judith Rascoe and David Rayfiel and directed by Sydney Pollack, and released by Universal Pictures. Lorenz's 1973 paper was 'Predictability: Does the Flap of a Butterfly's Wings in Brazil set off a Tornado in Texas?', a title that the shy and exacting Lorenz owed to a colleague, Philip Merilees; Lorenz was going to go with 'a seagull causing a storm'.

16   Lorenz quoted in Steven H. Strogatz , *Nonlinear Dynamics and*

ENDNOTES

Chaos: With Applications to Physics, Biology, Chemistry, and Engineering, CRC Press, (2nd Ed) 2015, Boca Raton, p.3.

17   Benoit B. Mandelbrot, *The Fractal Geometry of Nature*, W.H. Freeman and Co., New York (1977), 1983, 'Restatement of Goals', p.58.

18   For an understanding of these terms see books by Melanie Mitchell, Steven Strogatz, M. Mitchell Waldrop or John H. Holland and Stephen Wolfram. I won't do them a terrible injustice by trying to summarise them here!

19   See especially the work of John Horgan, particularly *The End of Science: Facing the Limits of Knowledge in the Twilight of the Scientific Age*, Broadway Books, New York, 1996.

20   Herbert A. Simon, 'The Architecture of Complexity', *Proceedings of the American Philosophical Society*, Vol. 106, No. 6., 1962, pp.467–482.

21   Summer Ash,'Astrophysicist Mario Livio on the intersection of art and science', *Smithsonian Magazine*, 7 September 2016; available online: http://www.smithsonianmag.com/science-nature/astrophysicist-mario-livio-intersection-art-and-science-180960334/#pB1pWd3QZQuICgtm.99/

22   A phrase employed by C.P. Snow in a lecture series that especially incensed literary critic F.R. Leavis. For more see C.P. Snow, *The Two Cultures*, Stefan Collini (intro.), Cambridge University Press, Cambridge, (1959) 1993; and F.R. Leavis, *The Two Cultures? The Significance of C.P. Snow*, Stefan Collini (intro.), Cambridge University Press, Cambridge, (1962) 2013. See also Julian Meyrick, 'Two Cultures (Again): Revisiting Leavis and Snow', *Sydney Review of Books*, 19 August, 2016; available online—https://sydneyreviewofbooks.com/essay/two-cultures-again-revisiting-leavis-and-snow/

23   From a notebook entry 24 July 1916, quoted in Nicholas F. Gier, 'Wittgenstein and Forms of Life', *Philosophy of the Social Sciences*, Vol. 10, 1980, p.248.

24   Nancy Cartwright, *The Dappled World: A Study of the Boundaries of Science*, Cambridge University Press, Cambridge, 1999, p.14. For more see: Stephan Hartmann, Carl Hoefer, and Luc Bovens (eds.), *Nancy Cartwright's Philosophy of Science*, Routledge, New York, 2008; Stephen H. Kellert, Helen E. Longino and C. Kenneth Waters (eds.), *Scientific Pluralism*, University of Minnesota, Minneapolis, 2006; Margaret Morrison, *Reconstructing Reality: Models, Mathematics and Simulations*, Oxford University Press, Oxford, 2015; Stéphanie Ruphy, *Scientific Pluralism Reconsidered: A New Approach to the (Dis)Unity of Science*, University of Pittsburgh Press, Pittsburgh, 2016.

25   This conceit—perhaps best known because of British physicist Arthur Eddington (who wrote about it in 1928), or French mathematician Émile Borel (similarly, in 1913) but also perhaps Jorge Luis Borges, Isaac Asimov or Kurt Vonnegut—runs that an infinite number of monkeys with typewriters will eventually generate the works of Shakespeare. A brief history of the idea was provided by Terry Butler in 2007 ('Monkeying around with text', January 2007, http://projects.chass.utoronto.ca/chwp/

CHC2005/Butler/Butler.htm) but scientists in the UK also tried the experiment with six monkeys in 2002 ('No words to describe monkeys' play', 9 May 2003, http://news.bbc.co.uk/2/hi/3013959.stm), with the macaques mostly just typing the letter 's'.

www.ingramcontent.com/pod-product-compliance
Lightning Source LLC
Chambersburg PA
CBHW040306170426
43194CB00022B/2920